The Arno Press Cinema Program

AN HISTORICAL
AND DESCRIPTIVE ANALYSIS
OF THE "WHY WE FIGHT" SERIES
With a New Introduction

Thomas William Bohn

ARNO PRESS

A New York Times Company

New York / 1977

This volume was selected for the
Dissertations on Film Series
of the ARNO PRESS CINEMA PROGRAM
by Garth S. Jowett, University of
Windsor, Canada

Editorial Supervision: Leslie Ike

First publication in book form, 1977,
by Arno Press Inc.

THE ARNO PRESS CINEMA PROGRAM
For complete listing of cinema titles see last pages

Manufactured in the United States of America

———•———

Library of Congress Cataloging in Publication Data

Bohn, Thomas W
    An historical and descriptive analysis of the
"Why we fight" series.

    (The Arno Press cinema program) (Dissertations
on film series)
    Originally presented as the author's thesis,
University of Wisconsin, 1968.
    Bibliography: p.
    1. World War, 1939-1945, in motion pictures.
2. Moving-pictures in propaganda. 3. Capra,
Frank, 1897-   4. Why we fight series (Motion
picture) I. Title. II. Series: Dissertations
on film series.
D743.23.B63   1977   791.43'53   74-40779
ISBN 0-405-09885-5

AN HISTORICAL AND DESCRIPTIVE ANALYSIS OF THE

"WHY WE FIGHT" SERIES

BY

THOMAS WILLIAM BOHN

A thesis submitted in partial fulfillment of the
requirements for the degree of

DOCTOR OF PHILOSOPHY
(Speech)

at the

UNIVERSITY OF WISCONSIN

1968

INTRODUCTION

"Interviews were attempted with other individuals
associated with the series, particularly Frank
Capra. However, Mr. Capra did not reply to the
seven letters asking for his assistance. Mr.
Tiomkin stated in an interview that Capra was
writing an autobiography and didn't want to divulge
any information which might prove publishable."

Almost 10 years have passed since this author's

graduate student frustration and helplessness was at its

peak. Mr. Capra was indeed writing his autobiography;

Frank Capra The Name Above the Title was published in

1971. I remember distinctly my feeling of uneasiness as

I began to read Capra's account of the "Why We Fight"

series. I had been very careful in trying to piece

together a reasonably accurate history of the series,

but was aware that a major source of information was

missing. My fears were groundless. Outside of a few

minor historical footnotes, Capra's account of his work

coincided directly with my findings. The one element

missing was Capra's personal running battle with the

Army establishment, in particular, various "lead-tailed"

Colonels who always seemed to get in his way. Capra's

recounting of the series falls in line with his book's,

title and central thesis - The Name Above the Title.

He overcame all odds and despite the Army made the films

his way.

Frankly, I was disappointed at the lack of personal

analysis by Capra. He seemed more intent on documenting

his battles with and triumphs over Army mediocrity than

in providing any fresh insights into the films themselves.

What has the hindsight and perspective of 10 years provided? Simply, a reaffirmation of the strength, vitality and lasting influence of the "Why We Fight" series. Despite subsequent attempts at "Why Korea" and "Why Vietnam" films, the "Why We Fight" series remains as one of the single best filmic examples of military orientation/propaganda ever produced. Its influence remains strong even today as reflected in two powerful films, The Sorrow and the Pity and Hearts and Minds. Although unique and original in their own right, these films clearly reveal the heritage of "Why We Fight" as they use "the truth" of filmed reality to convince and persuade. As Capra stated in his auto-biography concerning his efforts to arrive at a seminal concept for the series:

> "What was the truth about this World War? Well,
> it was obvious to me that the Nazis of Germany...
> were out to deliberately take over the free
> nations by force so they could stamp out human
> freedom and establish their own world dictator-
> ship... But how did I know that statement was
> true? Who proved it to me? Why, the enemy
> himself proved it to me, in his acts, his books,
> his speeches, his films.

Although perhaps concerned with different enemies, The Sorrow and the Pity and Hearts and Minds both reflect Capra's thinking; thinking that forms the basic essence and strength of the compilation form.

Thomas W. Bohn
Evansville, Ind.
August 16, 1976

ACKNOWLEDGMENTS

I wish to express my gratitude to Professor L. W. Lichty for his guidance throughout the preparation of this thesis.

A special note of gratitude and appreciation to Professor Ordean Ness for his insight and, above all, his patience and good humor in what must have been at times a trying experience.

I also wish to thank the Graduate School of the University of Wisconsin for providing financial aid which made the completion of this thesis possible.

And, of course, to my wife Mary, for her sense of values, and her dedication to a cause which must have seemed at times a bit remote.

TABLE OF CONTENTS

Page

ACKNOWLEDGMENTS . . . .

LIST OF TABLES . . . .

Chapter

I. INTRODUCTION AND BACKGROUND   1

   PURPOSE   1

   JUSTIFICATION OF PROBLEM AREA   2

   MATERIALS   4

      Historical   4

      Analysis   5

   REVIEW OF LITERATURE   7

   DEFINITIONS AND BACKGROUND   10

      Definition   10

   HISTORY   16

      Pre-Documentary Developments   17

      Development of Documentary   19

   METHODOLOGY   26

   ORGANIZATION OF REMAINDER OF DISSERTATION   28

   FOOTNOTES   29

II. THE DOCUMENTARY FILM IN WAR   33

   WORLD WAR I   33

      Civilian   34

      Military   38

Chapter   Page

       POST WORLD WAR I   40

       PRE-WORLD WAR II BUILDUP   40

          Military   40

          Civilian   41

       WORLD WAR II   42

          Civilian   42

          Military   48

          Foreign and Overseas Documentary   67

          Wartime Documentary Abroad   71

          United States Commercial   72

       SUMMARY   74

          Themes   75

       FOOTNOTES   78

III. A HISTORY OF THE "WHY WE FIGHT" SERIES   86

       INCREASED EMPHASIS ON THE NEED FOR MORALE   86

          History of Morale Activity in the Armed Forces .   90

       THE "WHY WE FIGHT" SERIES   95

          Background   95

          Beginning   96

          Purposes and Objectives   98

          Organization of the Film Unit   101

          Personnel   102

          Production   104

          Distribution   107

Chapter   Page

          Use   108

          Criticism-Reaction   110

     FOOTNOTES   116

IV. THEMES OF THE "WHY WE FIGHT" SERIES   121

     INTRODUCTION   121

     PRESENTATION OF THEMES   122

          Explication   122

          Contrast   129

     THEMES   131

          Free World   132

          Slave World   145

          The Allies   149

     SUMMARY AND CONCLUSIONS   155

V.   SOUND   157

     INTRODUCTION   157

     SPEECH   158

          Narration   158

          Natural Speech   168

     NATURAL SOUNDS   173

          Characteristics   174

          Function   175

     MUSIC   177

          Form   177

         Characteristics 179

         Functions 181

    SUMMARY 186

    FOOTNOTES 189

VI. VISUAL STYLE 190

    INTRODUCTION 190

         Definitions 190

    ELEMENTS OF VISUAL STRUCTURE 194

         Intra-Shot Elements 195

         Inter-Shot Elements 216

         Editing 227

    SUMMARY 230

    FOOTNOTES 233

VII. SUMMARY AND DISCUSSION 234

    BASIC FOCUS OF THE STUDY 234

    SUMMARY AND DISCUSSION 234

         History 234

         Themes 239

         Sound 241

         Visual Style 243

         Final Conclusions 246

    LIMITATIONS OF THE STUDY 250

    IMPLICATIONS FOR FURTHER RESEARCH 251

    FOOTNOTES 253

BIBLIOGRAPHY 254

LIST OF TABLES

Table	Page
I	200
II	205
III	210
IV	213
V	216
VI	223

CHAPTER I

INTRODUCTION AND BACKGROUND

"The "Why We Fight" series deserves close examination by students of film technique."[1]

PURPOSE

This statement by Richard Griffith, noted film critic and chief researcher for the "Why We Fight" series, postulates a need. This study attempts to meet that need. The purposes of this study are to provide a history and description of the "Why We Fight" series and to analyze the films in the series as artistic creations. The essential question of this study is: What are the characteristic elements and qualities of the "Why We Fight" films and how do they function as elements of filmic construction?

Thus, the study has two separate areas of emphasis. The first area outlines the history and function of the documentary film in war and provides a history and description of the "Why We Fight" series and its place in the Army film program. This portion functions as a frame of reference for the analysis of the films themselves. The second area analyzes the thematic and structural characteristics of the films themselves. This portion of the study does not attempt to ascertain the meanings of the structural elements and patterns found in the films. Nor does it attempt to fit the film material into a preconceived theory

1

of communication. Rather, it is an identification and analysis of the structural elements and patterns found in the films. The films have been labeled propaganda. An attempt could have been made to fit the filmic elements into a theory of persuasion. However, it is necessary that the data, the structural elements themselves, not be forced into any particular theory. They should be allowed to emerge freely from the films.

JUSTIFICATION OF PROBLEM AREA

Justification for this study arises from the fact that although the "Why We Fight" series has been consistently referred to by critics as "outstanding" and "brilliant," although it is called the finest documentary work to emerge from World War II, there has been no previous study, popular or academic, devoted to it. (Hovland, Lumsdaine and Sheffield reported their research on the effects of the first four films in the series in Experiments on Mass Communication.) Justification also arises out of the research method itself as this study is the first to apply a particular research method to sound film.

There is ample evidence that the "Why We Fight" series is accorded high critical esteem. Richard Griffith states that "The formidable power of the film medium can be seen at its source in the elementary examples of the effects to be gained by the composition of images in counterpoint with sound, music and speech."[2] Griffith also states, "That they, or such adaptations of them as perspective suggests should be shown and shown again and that more films like them are desperately needed is as painfully evident."[3] This statement, made in 1952, was precipitated by the dearth in documentary film in the postwar years.

Karel Reisz states, "The Americans have developed their own vigorous
polemical style of compilation . . . reaching a peak of achievement in
'The March of Time' films and Frank Capra's war-time 'Why We Fight'
series."[4] Jay Leyda, in his book on compilation film, Films Beget
Films, states, "Their series of seven feature-length films, 'Why We
Fight', was the most instructive body of compilation to come out of the
war."[5] Leyda states further that

> . . . The Battle of Russia was cut so brilliantly
> that it was studied and greatly admired in the Soviet
> Union--the only American film reflection of the Soviet
> front that required no apology. It is the only known
> instance in the war where one country's films, as cut
> by another country's editors, were acknowledged happily
> by the country of their origin.[6]

Burton Benjamin in his forward to A. William Bluem's book, Documentary
in American Television, states:

> Dr. Bluem freely recognizes the documentarian's debt
> to his predecessors. It is high time some of the
> practitioners in the field do so. To give one example,
> the next producer who cuts a rousing war sequence and
> does not admit some small debt to Frank Capra and 'Why
> We Fight' is probably not playing fair. His World War
> II series has been an inspiration to creative people,
> particularly film editors, ever since.[7]

Justification for this study also arises out of the research
method. Although the method of film analysis employed in this study
is not new, it has been rarely used. Only four previously existing
studies utilizing detailed shot analysis as the major research method
are known to this writer. They are Theodore Huff's analysis of The
Birth of a Nation and Intolerance, John B. Kuiper's analysis of the
four silent films of S. M. Eisenstein and Richard B. Byrne's analysis
of German expressionist films. To this writer's knowledge, no study
of a sound film utilizing the method of detailed shot analysis has

been conducted. Sound poses some interesting questions to the researcher utilizing shot analysis. It is not enough to note the visual patterns and attempt to ascertain their function in terms of visual criteria only. Sound must and does play an important role, not only in the relationship to the visual structure of the film, but as a strong independent element. Further method justification arises from a statement made by Byrne in his study.

> One is unable to place the films accurately in their proper stylistic perspective since comparable figures are not available for other film genres. When studies similar to the present one have been completed for the films of other periods and styles, the portions of the present study entailing analysis by tabulation and measurement will increase in value.[8]

A similar statement can be made regarding those portions of this study involving tabulation and measurement, although the comparison would be most fruitful with other sound documentaries.

MATERIALS

Historical

Historical data in this study were used for three basic purposes: (1) To provide a proper framework for the "Why We Fight" series in the history of the documentary film movement, (2) To provide a more specific framework for the "Why We Fight" series as wartime documentary, (3) To provide a history of the production of the films, including information on personnel, materials, production, use and distribution.

This information was gathered from many sources. The resources of the National Archives in Washington, D.C., were the primary source of data concerning the documentary film in war and the history of the "Why We Fight" series itself. Much of the research here involved a page by page review of innumerable and often irrelevant memos, letters and manuscripts. Other material was gathered at the University of Wisconsin Library, the Wisconsin State Historical Library in Madison and The Library of Congress in Washington. Other standard indices were consulted for information, including Readers Guide and The New York Times Index, among others.

Several books and magazines were particularly helpful in this research. The Film Till Now by Paul Rotha and Richard Griffith, and Documentary Film by Paul Rotha, Sinclair Road and Richard Griffith are two standard historical sources in film and provided general information on the history and development of the documentary film. Film News, a magazine devoted to documentary and educational motion pictures, was an especially valuable source regarding the civilian and military documentary in war. One other magazine, Business Screen, was especially helpful concerning the documentary film in war. Two special issues were published in 1945. One reviewed the activity of the Army Pictorial Service and the other was a report on the training film activity of the United States Navy. This writer is indebted to Mr. O. H. Coelln, editor and publisher of Business Screen, for sending gratis, the special hard-to-obtain issues. Finally, two official Army manuscripts, The Signal Corps Army Pictorial Service in World War II and A Study of Information and Education Activities in World War II, provided a wealth of specific data regarding the use of film by the Army during World War II.

Analysis

The major source of material for analysis was, of course, the films themselves. Five of the films, Prelude to War, The Nazis Strike,

The Battle of Britain, The Battle of Russia and War Comes to America,
were available at the Bureau of Audio-Visual Instruction at the
University of Wisconsin. Through the help of Mr. Andrew Holmes these
films were made available to the writer for long periods of time in
order to conduct the detailed analysis necessary. Divide and Conquer
was obtained from The Department of Defense. The Battle of China was
available for viewing only at The National Archives. Detailed shot
analysis sheets were constructed for all of these films except The
Battle of China and The Battle of Russia. These sheets formed the
basis for the visual analysis of the films. In addition, the sound
tracks of all of the films were recorded at The National Archives.

Other primary analysis data included shooting scripts for all of
the films except War Comes to America. These were collected at The
National Archives.

A final source of both analytical and historical data was personal
interviews and correspondence. Of particular help were personal interviews with Colonel Dallas W. Hoadley, Deputy for Training Materials,
U. S. Army and Mr. Dimitri Tiomkin, well-known Hollywood music composer
and composer for the "Why We Fight" films. Interviews were attempted
with other individuals associated with the series, particularly Frank
Capra. However, Mr. Capra did not reply to the seven letters asking
for his assistance. Mr. Tiomkin stated in an interview that Capra was
writing an autobiography and didn't want to divulge any information
which might prove publishable. Individuals, such as Eric Knight,
Anthony Veiller and Walter Huston, are deceased. Other individuals,
such as Colonel R. C. Barret (Retired), who was in charge of the Army

Pictorial Center and Mr. Wingate Smith, closely associated with the series, refused to be interviewed. (It might be noted in a personal aside that research involving the military and Hollywood seems to be a dangerous combination. Too many individuals are either too busy or unwilling to cooperate.)

REVIEW OF LITERATURE

The motion picture has always been a source of popular study. Fan magazines and newspaper and magazine articles and reviews have existed almost from the beginning of the theatrical distribution of the motion picture. Film scholarship, on the other hand, is relatively recent.

Film scholarship can and does take several directions. There is first of all historical research. Typical examples of scholarly study in this area are: Raymond Fielding's "History of the March of Time"; Robert Snyder's "A History of the Early Productions of Pare Lorentz and the United States Film Service, 1935-1940"; and Richard Sanderson's "A Historical Study of the Development of American Motion Picture Content and Technique Prior to 1904."[9]

Critical and descriptive studies are another form of film scholarship. Examples in this area include: Donald Fernow's "The Treatment of Social Problems in the Entertainment Film"; John Kuiper's "Pictorial Composition in the Cinema"; and James Seiger's "An Analysis of Catholic Censorship of Motion Picture Films in the United States."[10]

There are, of course, experimental studies relating to film. Examples in this area include: Charles Palmer's "The Use of Sound Motion Pictures in the Measurement of Speech Skills"; and Hoyt

Griffith's "An Experimental Investigation to Determine the Instructional and Persuasive Effects of Film Music in an Educational Film."[11]

The largest area of film scholarship occurs in the general area
of critical/evaluative research. Typical of the numerous studies in
this field are: Terry Theodore's "The Negro In Hollywood: A Critical
Study of Entertainment Films Containing Negro Themes"; Joseph Richen's
"An Analysis of Four Manuscripts of Ingmar Bergman"; and Robert Kanter's
"A Critical Survey of the Use of Creative Sound in Motion Pictures."[12]

There are other research studies in film which could be mentioned.
However, it is not the intention of this portion of the study to account
for all forms of motion picture research. This brief review functions
as a brief outline of the breakdown in topic area in film scholarship
and some of the typical research done in each area.

Studies related specifically to this one in method or content
are few. No previous studies were found devoted to any aspect of the
"Why We Fight" series, except the accounts of the research conducted
by the Information and Education Division published in Experiments On
Mass Communication by Hovland, Lumsdaine and Sheffield. Their research
involved only the first four films of the series and was devoted exclusively to an experimental investigation into the effects of the films.
This work was a part of the research done on several orientation and
training films, and was not devoted exclusively to the "Why We Fight"
series. The results of their investigation are spelled out in greater
detail in Chapter III.

Previous studies utilizing the basic research method employed in
this study have already been mentioned. However, the basic focus of

each of these studies should be outlined. Theodore Huff's analysis of
The Birth of a Nation and Intolerance was intended to provide a detailed
description of the films and their characteristics. He looked at the
various elements of filmic construction as they emerged from the films
and incorporated them into his description of the films. John Kuiper's
analysis of the four silent films of S. M. Eisenstein was conducted in
order to determine the relationships that exist between the cinematic
construction of the films and the meanings expressed by them. He
identified two broad types of passages in the films, figurative and
narrative. He concluded that the films construct a visual texture of
meaning that challenges the understanding. Richard Byrne's study of
German expressionistic films aimed at discovering the characteristic
elements and qualities of the films. He also tested the validity of
the relationship between expressionism in the films and other media.
His study concentrated on the elements of decor, lighting and acting
and the role they played in the films.

Previous studies treating documentary film in general and in
World War II are more numerous but there is no overabundance. Reviewing
all of them, despite their relatively small number, would be tedious and
serve no purpose. Those most specifically related to the "Why We Fight"
series are: Charles Pillow's "Survey of Documentary and Technical Cine
Photography at the Air Force Flight Test Center"; Peter Drown's "An
Investigation into the Evolution of Motion Picture Photography and
Film Usage in the United States Marine Corps, 1940-1945"; Ross Vincent's
"Historical Study of the Army Air Force's First Motion Picture Unit
(18th AAFEC) in World War II"; Merle Lewey's "Historical and Operational

Record Films in the Department of the Army"; Paul Myatt's "A Survey of

the Use of Motion Pictures in Flight Training by the United States

Navy"; and Richard MacCann's "Documentary Film and Democratic Govern-

ment: An Administrative History from Pare Lorentz to John Huston."[13]

DEFINITIONS AND BACKGROUND

Definition

Before embarking on a historical review of the documentary film,

a need exists to define the subject under discussion and to set forth

its basic method and approach. This is not an easy task. Seemingly,

every film critic and historian, as well as "experts" in sociology,

history and art, have undertaken a definition of "documentary." Each

one has postulated his own definition, or at least so it seems.

The word "documentary" to describe a particular film, film style

or approach was introduced by John Grierson in the early 1920's. It is

derived from the French word "documentaire," meaning travel films.[14]

Since Grierson first penned the word, definitions of documentary

have ranged all the way from Grierson's general and inclusive "creative

treatment of actuality" to the complex and somewhat exclusive

> . . . realistic portrayal, in depth, of a contemporary-
> or past-culture or situation; . . . with its purpose
> being to supply background material and unbiased social
> information, as it relates to history, geography,
> customs and mores.[15]

In between, are myriad other meanings and interpretations.

Basically, the definition of documentary film falls into four

categories: (1) Subject matter/content, (2) Method/approach, (3)

Aesthetic principles, (4) Intent or purpose. The first and last categories are by far the most popular, despite Richard MacCann's statement that people who write about documentary either emphasize method or content.[16] When most theorists and/or critics discussed method they were usually referring to purpose or intent. Little concrete material was found setting forth explicit methods or approaches to documentary.

Subject Matter/Content

Subject matter/content-oriented theorists generally stress a type or types of films as being "documentary." Waldron, in The Information Film, includes under her definition of documentary "all serious non-theatrical films."[17] The Academy of Motion Picture Arts and Sciences defines documentary films as "those dealing with significant historical, scientific or economic subjects. . . ."[18] Other definitions include: "a film that portrays real people in a real social situation,"[19] "a film that attempts to make some point about real life and support its contention with convincing evidence . . . ,"[20] and "films based on real life experiences using no sets and no professional actors."[21] As Robert Katz stated: "The documentary medium must have room for many categories of film."[22] Hugh Baddeley includes teaching in the classroom and recordings under documentary. He states that the "factual film" is a more concrete and appropriate term than documentary.[23] All of these definitions, as concrete and explicit as some of them try to be, fall short of a complete understanding of the documentary film. Documentary is not merely a specific type of content or subject. It must and does include more.

Method/Approach

Noted documentarian, Roy Stryker, states that "documentary is an approach, not a technique. . . ." He spoke of a documentary "attitude" which provides for the elements of a film and gives it certain limitations and provides direction.[24] Richard MacCann feels that documentary is chiefly an approach to art or life rather than a specific technique for its execution.[25] But just exactly what this method or approach is, seems to escape complete definition. On the one hand, Paul Rotha states that the documentary method is a method of "philosophic reasoning."[26] This would seem to put him in the propaganda-conscious camp of Eisenstein. John Grierson, the other key figure in British and later Canadian documentary, states that in documentary you do not shoot with your head only, but also with your stomach muscles.[27] Another attempt at definition states that the documentary method involves making a point about real life, and supporting its contention with convincing evidence.[28] William Bluem states that what distinguishes documentary's approach ". . . is the involvement of the viewer in the human significance of events."[29] Rotha sums up this "school" of thought by his comment that documentary determines the approach to a subject, but not necessarily the subject itself.[30] The advocates of the "method" definition of documentary continually stress the approach of the film-maker. They state that the subject does not determine the method used or whether a film is documentary or not. Rather, the approach itself is the defining element of documentary. However, few theorists attempt any concrete "stab" at formulating a clear conception of just what is this approach. When forced back to clear-cut concepts, many seem to hedge with statements about "philosophic reasoning" and "gut shooting." This "approach" philosophy seems to find some clearness and distinction when it is allied with the two remaining methods of definition, aesthetic elements and purpose.

Aesthetic Elements

Many of the approach theorists clarify their stand by naming "elements" which make up the documentary. This still does not, however, "define" the approach or method of working with these elements. Grierson states, in what is perhaps the most universally recognized definition of documentary, that documentary is the "creative treatment of actuality."[31] Rotha states that the essence of the documentary method lies in the dramatization of actual material. Documentary is truthful, according to Rotha, only when it implies a particular attitude of mind toward a subject. The documentary method is not fixed, it is complex. It is contemporary fact and event expressed in relation to human association.[32] Rotha also sets forth "four traditions" of documentary: (1) the naturalist, (2) the realist, (3) the newsreel, (4) the propagandist.[33] These traditions reflect his emphasis on attitude or method. Each of these "traditions" is characterized by a different approach to the film, not by any particular subject-matter or content. It is the elements of each of these approaches which distinguish them from each other.

William Bluem also comments upon the aesthetic elements in documentary. He states that the function of documentary is to make drama from life.[34] Waldron states: "It is the spirit of the film rather than the actual form which determines whether it uses the documentary approach or not."[35] The elements of this spirit, according to Waldron,

are sincerity, realism, an eye for detail, a probing for hidden meanings
and the awareness of the essential qualities of things and people.[36]

There is within the aesthetic approach a concern for dramatization;
the interpretation in dramatic form of the actuality surrounding man.
Once again, little is said regarding the elements which make up this
dramatization of reality. As in the "method" approach, it is the
artist himself who determines the elements. Most of the theorists
writing about documentary are or were makers of documentary films as
well as critics. This may in part explain their vagueness. They may
"feel" the approach and the drama, and "know" the elements which make
up such drama. However, they perhaps find them difficult to verbalize
and also do not want to risk excluding any element. Thus, the aesthetic
elements, as in the approach, are rarely spelled out.

Purpose/Intent

This last approach to defining documentary exhibits the most
concreteness and agreement. As Cecile Starr stated: "The documentary
film must have a purpose, a direction."[37] Surprisingly, many theorists
agree on what should be this purpose. John Grierson believes persuasion
is the documentary purpose.[38] Paul Rotha states that the essential purpose of documentary lies in the ends applied to the observation of the
documentary camera, not the observation itself. He states that a
documentary film-maker is a "propagandist making use of the most influential instrument of his time."[39] Indeed, Rotha excludes Flaherty's
"idyllic" films, Ruttman's Berlin and the "art for art's sake" approach
it represents and the newsreel tradition from the mainstream of documentar

film. They all may have contributed to the ultimate creation of "true"
documentary, but none of them typifies the essence of the documentary
approach. Irving Jacoby almost echoes Rotha's exclusions by stating
that the purpose of influencing is the documentary's reason for existing.
We must, according to Jacoby, measure documentary films by the achievement of this purpose.[40] Hugh Baddeley comments that documentary is a
tool, an instrument with a thousand serious jobs to do.[41] William
Bluem states that documentary seeks to inform, but above all, it seeks
to influence. "Communication is valid as documentary only when it is
designed to further and advance individual and social causes, values,
conditions, and institutions by inspiring man to consider their significance and relationship to himself as a social being."[42] Rotha, like
Bluem, concludes that documentary films have certain elements in common:
(1) each deals with attitudes and values, (2) each deals with some problem of the individual's adjustment to the world, (3) each seeks to motivate the individual.[43]

Summary

What patterns or conclusions arise out of this review? Taking
qualities of meaning from all four forms of definition, the documentary
film, as Grierson and Rotha in particular observe, emerges as a social
statement, using actuality as its theme and persuasion as its goal.
This may be a somewhat narrow definition. However, it does encompass
the main stream of thought regarding the documentary film. Rotha
observes that documentary is complex.[44] Grierson said it is a clumsy
definition.[45] It is all of this and more. Any attempt to pinpoint

the exact nature, method, theme or approach of documentary seems fruit-
less. Documentary is an approach to film that presumes actuality as
its theme and persuasion as its goal. It is, above all, a social
statement. Certain factual films fall within this framework, others
do not. That the "Why We Fight" series does, there seems to be little
doubt.

HISTORY

A review of the history and development of the documentary film
reveals that the term does not enjoy universal agreement. It grew out
of many traditions. In the broad sense of "factual, social purpose"
film as differentiated from fictional entertainment film, it encompasses
a great many types of film. However, documentary in the "classical"
sense refers to a specific type of film, film as a social statement
with a specific persuasive goal in mind. This eliminates many of the
"nuts and bolts" training and instructional films so prevalent during
World War II and in the classroom. As Richard Griffith correctly observed: "Most of the films of World War II did not fall under this
category [documentary film]."[46] Only a few, such as the "Why We Fight"
series and some of the historical campaign films like Memphis Belle,
came under the historic reading of documentary. However, in order to
provide a reasonably complete history and to trace the major lines of
development of the "Why We Fight" series, other forms and types of
films will be described and discussed.

It does not seem necessary to delve too deeply into the history
and development of the documentary film. Most of the information is
readily available in numerous secondary sources, most of which are

cited here. This chapter functions as a frame of reference for the "Why We Fight" series and its chronological place in the documentary film movement, not as a definitive history of the documentary film. Therefore, only the broadest outline will be utilized, tracing just the major developments.

Pre-Documentary Developments

From the beginning, the cinema was utilized for non-fictional purposes. The very first pictures by Edison and the Lumiere brothers, among others, were of real events and real people. There were travel films, sports films, scientific films, and of course, newsreels. However, none of these forms went beyond merely recording events in their natural environment. It was essentially the development of the story film by Porter, Griffith and others, coupled with the already present use of film to record actual events, that gave birth to the documentary film. Rotha observed that the documentary film did not appear as a distinctive method of film-making at any given moment in the cinema with any particular production, but rather evolved over a period of time.[47] Developments in several countries in the 1920's contributed toward a concept of documentary film. Flaherty in America, Vertov in Russia, Ruttmann in Germany, Cavalcanti in France and Grierson in Britain all helped to develop the documentary film into a distinct form.

It is difficult to set specific times and films dating the documentary film movement. However, most theorists agree that the basic roots of documentary began in 1922 with Robert Flaherty's Nanook of the North. Flaherty was the first to explore on film the nature of man in relation to his natural environment in a way suggesting something more than the mere recording of actuality. Flaherty probed deeply into the relationship of the Eskimo to his environment and presented a study of this phenomena on film. Flaherty went on to produce another such study in Moana in 1926. Although Flaherty sowed the seed of the documentary movement, his was but one approach. Other forms and theories were being experimented with in other countries.

In Russia, Dziga Vertov began to make films based upon his theory that the camera has the power of the human eye to penetrate every detail of contemporary life. Further work by Eisenstein, Pudovkin and Dovjenko utilizing the epic form, and Esther Schub in her pioneering work with the compilation form influenced the approach of documentary in the West. Other significant developments occurred in Germany and France where Walther Ruttmann and Alberto Cavalcanti created impressionistic studies of life in the city.

However, the documentary film cannot be traced directly from any of these traditions. Flaherty's films had no real social purpose in mind. They were essentially idyllic ballads portraying the classic struggle of man and his environment. His approach could not effectively translate the problems of a modern urban industrial society into meaningful social statements. The Russians were essentially tied down to supporting ideologies, promoting achievement and recording progress. Little room was left for the basic interpretation so necessary for a true meaning of documentary. This was also true of Ruttmann and Cavalcanti. Their impressionistic studies of man in the city, while attempting to use film in a sociological way, appealed chiefly through

symbols to emotions and feeling. They did little to evoke understanding
and to stir up positive action in the pursuit of a specific purpose or
goal.

Development of Documentary
England

It was in England, mainly through the efforts of one man, that
the documentary film emerged as a powerful social instrument. This
beginning is the story of John Grierson. Grierson actually coined the
word documentary in a film review for a New York newspaper written
while he was in the United States studying public relations in 1926.[48]
He returned to Britain and in 1929, while working for the Empire Marketing Board, produced Drifters. It achieved little that was new or
would prove influential in a stylistic sense. Grierson's film, however,
laid the foundation for documentary in Britain and elsewhere as a filmic
form designed to influence, motivate and interpret the basic problems of
society in meaningful ways. The important and decisive difference of
Drifters was that here the factual film was being used to advance
specific goals and needs. The documentary film became a part of the
social process, stimulating, prodding, and above all, persuading.
Here for the first time, film was being used primarily as an instrument
of social progress; as a tool to achieve goals, solve problems and
influence needs and desires.

Through the 30's under the Empire Marketing Board and later the
General Post Office, Grierson, Henry Watt and Basil Wright, among
others, continued this tradition with such films as Night Mail, Song
of Ceylon and Coal Face.

With the coming war in 1939, the British had a solid tradition
of documentary film-making dating back ten years. Their war effort
in documentary, while not as prodigious as the United States, exhibited
the influence of this tradition.

Other Countries

Documentary film in other countries outside the United States
and Britain achieved little prominence and recognition. Russia exhibited the beginning of a documentary movement. However, the interests
of men such as Eisenstein, Pudovkin and Dovjenko did not lie in this
area. Also, the restriction on content and interpretation by the
Soviet government distilled the purpose of documentary.

France had the beginning force of the avante-garde, but this had
spent itself by the early 30's. Some distinctive films such as Vigo's
Zéro de Conduite in 1933 and L'Atalante in 1934 were produced. However,
as Rotha comments, "A clear and consistent expression of the realities
of the French scene were stifled."[49]

Germany had the early film efforts of Ruttmann. With the takeover of Hitler, any interpretation of German life outside of what he
desired became impossible. Two forms of realistic film did emerge
from Germany, however, before the war. The first was the "kulturfilm."
It consisted basically of travelogues, publicity features and "fascinating fact" film, the last of which, according to Rotha, was all
bad because it was concerned with the past or sidelines of life and
therefore not documentary.[50] The other was Leni Riefenstahl's Triumph
of the Will, followed by Olympia. The films were essentially a

glorification of Nazi mythology encompassing distorted events while
dealing with factual material. However, the style and technique of
the films, especially the strong editing, were notable.

Italy made some minor efforts beginning with the Instituto Luce
in 1925 which encouraged the production of scientific and educational
films.[51] However, as in Germany, with the advent of Mussolini, documentary ceased to function. The rise of neo-realism (actually not a
form of documentary, but often labeled as such) did not occur until
the closing year of the war.

Some work was done in the Netherlands by Joris Ivens and in
Denmark by Paul Henningsen and Theodor Christensen.

Canada embarked quite late on a documentary film program, but it
soon rivaled Britain and the United States. The National Film Act was
signed May 2, 1939, creating the National Film Board with John Grierson
as head. The Board produced many notable films, including the series
"The World in Action," termed by Rotha as among "the most remarkable
films of all time."[52]

Outside of Britain and the few minor examples just mentioned,
the documentary film did not achieve great prominence in the prewar
years with the notable exception of the United States.

United States

Aside from the early work of Flaherty and some of the "agitprop"
films of Stern and Ivens, the American documentary film had a relatively
late start. Again, specific dates and films are arbitrary, to say the
least. However, like Britain, the story of documentary film in the
United States up to World War II was essentially the story of one man,

Pare Lorentz. His 1936 production, The Plow That Broke the Plains, is generally acknowledged as the beginning of the American documentary film. There were other realist films made before this, but like Drifters, Lorentz's film pointed a way. Rotha comments that The Plow That Broke the Plains had vision and ambition, showed that the documentary film was no longer the monopoly of Europe, and, along with the second film, The River, did more to secure the popular recognition of the documentary film in America than any other picture.[53]

U.S. Film Service. The Plow That Broke the Plains, made for the Resettlement Administration, was the beginning of a brief productive "golden era" in American documentary film. The River was the next important documentary film to be produced. It achieved even more popularity and critical acclaim than The Plow That Broke the Plains. The success of Lorentz and his film unit focused attention on the documentary and resulted in the formation of a centralized government film service. In 1938, President Roosevelt instructed the Executive Director of the National Emergency Council to establish within his agency the United States Film Service.[54] The Service lasted a little over two years, but in that time produced a number of notable documentaries, including Ecce Homo, Lorentz's The Fight for Life, Flaherty's The Land and Joris Iven's Power and the Land. The Film Service acted as a coordinating agency for the film ideas of other government departments and a gathering place for top-flight documentary directors much like the EMB and the GPO in Britain. However, the Film Service and its work were always suspect to congressional inquiries investigating the "New Deal propaganda" it disseminated. Thus, on June 30, 1940, it passed out of existence.[55]

Despite the efforts of the Roosevelt administration through the
U.S. Film Service and other agencies, the U.S. documentary film came
into being largely through the efforts of isolated individuals.
Typical of the independent spirit of America, documentary in this
country before World War II was the story of individual endeavor with
nearly as many styles and purposes as individuals.

March of Time. One of the most important and influential innova-
tions affecting documentary began in 1935: It was a new concept in
screen journalism called "The March of Time." At first it stayed with
the normal six- to ten-subject format of the typical newsreel. However,
it soon changed to the production of two more-or-less in-depth features
and later to a single feature per issue. Here, the possibility of re-
enactment, always thought to be technique outside the scope of documentary, proved to be a valid instrument for the creation of vital
social statements. "The March of Time" burst out of its newsreel
beginning, and with such films as Inside Nazi Germany brought a new
dimension to the American film of fact. Many of the films of World
War II, including the "Why We Fight" series, owed a great deal in style
and technique to "The March of Time."

Pare Lorentz. Pare Lorentz rode the crest of the The Plow That
Broke the Plains and The River to popular success and was appointed
head of the U.S. Film Service. His approach to documentary, especially
in The River, was essentially poetic and symbolic. However, his films
differed from the early symbolism of Ruttmann and Cavalcanti. They
were primarily vehicles for social commentary and analysis. Lorentz's
"poetry" did not only sound and look good, it was also an instrument

of persuasion. Thus, it gained significance, rather than merely being art for art's sake.

Ralph Steiner and Willard Van Dyke. These two men collaborated on The City in 1940. Less romantic in appeal than the Lorentz films, it too had social commentary as its ultimate goal as it attempted to show man in a particular environment.

Joris Ivens. He produced The Spanish Earth, a film harsher in quality and displaying its propaganda much more than Lorentz. Ivens joined the U.S. Film Service and produced a memorable film, The Power and the Land.

Others. Other men and styles important to the development of documentary were: Frontier Films which produced several notable films, including Native Land; Herbert Kline, who focused his attention on the decisive events of the prewar period with results such as The Crisis in 1938 and Lights Out in Europe in 1939; John Ferna and his 1940 production And So They Live; Julien Bryan, world lecturer and film-maker; and Jules Bucher, Irving Lerner and Helen Van Dongen.[56]

Despite these and other individual accomplishments, the documentary film in America, after the demise of the U.S. Film Service in 1940, had little direction. Industry and education were both cautious because of limited budgets and the fear of being labeled producers and/ or sponsors of "New Deal propaganda." As Rotha states, "The little group of enthusiasts who constituted the American documentary 'movement' lacked salesmanship."[57] They also lacked an effective organization which would back their activity, and as Griffith points out, they lacked the personal desire to continue in a frustrating and unsure field

World War II solved many of these problems and gave American documentary film purpose and direction. There was immediate and almost universal agreement on goals and needs. The documentary film no longer could remain cautious. The goal was apparent and the documentary film enlisted for the duration.

The documentary film grew out of many traditions. It was first utilized as a means of exhibiting natural exteriors and real human beings in relation to this background. This approach achieved its ultimate form in the work of Robert Flaherty. Another influence was the aesthetic realism of Ruttmann and Cavalcanti. The newsreels also made a contribution, especially the specialized form of "The March of Time." The documentary film also grew out of a concern for and interest in propaganda as an important tool in national and international communication. This form was utilized best by Grierson and the British school of documentary.

All of these traditions and forms found a ready audience and willing producers in the atmosphere of World War II. None of the frustrating years of development before the war was wasted. Despite the many directions and individual styles and purposes, the documentary film of World War II experienced relatively little confusion and disorganization. Rather, the atmosphere of the time seemed to dictate a need and purpose which fused the many disparate elements together into an effective filmic force. The influence of "The March of Time," for example, can be clearly seen in the "Why We Fight" series. The feature-length films of Lorentz and Ivens, among others, influenced the histori-cal campaign films of Wyler, Ford and Huston. The "Army Navy Screen

Magazine" owes some degree of debt to "The March of Time." In Britain, the story was much the same.

World War II documentary utilized some specific styles and techniques of prewar documentary, but owed its biggest debt to a tradition, a movement and attitude created out of the tireless efforts of many individuals and organizations. Above all, the concept of using film for strong social purpose, for presenting the problems of man in a realistic light, and most of all for persuasion and propaganda was the most valuable influence the documentary film movement and its creators gave.

The story of the documentary film up to World War II is a story of groping, of problems, of frustration and of persistence. Much of this early story would change with the advent of war and its desperate needs and goals. Chapter II reviews in some detail the documentary in war, including the men who created it, the forms and styles it encompassed and the purposes it served.

METHODOLOGY

Richard Byrne has outlined the basic research methodology used in his study of German expressionist films in an article in Speech Monographs.[59] The same approach was utilized by John Kuiper in his analysis of the four silent films of S. M. Eisenstein and Theodore Huff in his analysis of The Birth of a Nation. This basic pattern has also been utilized in this study. Byrne and Kuiper both correctly observe that film is a dynamic medium. Repeated projections are not sufficient in order to make accurate judgments about the complex nature of the film medium. A more analytical method is needed.

This method is the detailed study of the films themselves. Written material was used only as clarifying and supporting material. As John Kuiper stated, "In method, the study started with the films. It is confined and limited primarily by what can be understood about the visual nature of a film presentation."[60]

All of the films except The Battle of China and The Battle of Russia were examined on a hand viewer. The Battle of China was not available for analysis, although it was viewed several times at The National Archives; a detailed shooting script was available on The Battle of Russia. Work sheets were assembled on which each shot was recorded in numerical sequence. Included on these sheets were shot length, camera angle, lens angle, camera movement, content of shot, transitions and special optical effects. Thus, the films were analyzed for elements making up the individual shot and also for editing techniques that established patterns and relationships between shots.

These work sheets formed what can be likened to detailed shooting scripts which provided the basis for the film analysis. Criteria on the function and uses of the filmic elements were derived from the writings of such critics and theorists as Arnheim, Spottiswoode, Reisz, Kuiper and Byrne, as well as personal observation. These criteria are described in detail in Chapter VI.

The research and the researcher were governed by film content. Categories were devised to encompass the evidence encountered. Thus, the research did not involve the filling in of predetermined slots of content or structure.

The sound tracks were also analyzed. They were separately re-corded and roughly aligned with the shot sequences on the work sheets. This enabled the researcher to establish basic audio-visual relation-ships in the films. The sound tracks were listened to separately as well, in order to isolate specific elements of style and technique.

Finally, each of the films except The Battle of China was viewed specifically for each of the separate visual elements in the films. This involved a minimum of eight separate viewings per film.

ORGANIZATION OF REMAINDER OF DISSERTATION

The dissertation is roughly divided into two sections. The first section covering Chapters II and III provides a history and description of the documentary film at war, and the "Why We Fight" series itself. The second section covering Chapters IV, V and VI is devoted to an analysis of the films themselves. Chapter IV treats the themes of the series, Chapter V analyzes the sound track and Chapter VI analyzes the visual style of the films. Each of the analysis chapters is divided into two major sections. The first describes the use and character-istics of the elements under discussion. The second analyzes the function performed by these elements. Chapter VII is a summary and commentary.

FOOTNOTES - CHAPTER I

[1]Paul Rotha and Richard Griffith, The Film Till Now (London: Spring Books, 1967), p. 462.

[2]Ibid.

[3]Paul Rotha, Sinclair Road, and Richard Griffith, Documentary Film (New York: Hastings House, 1963), p. 351.

[4]Karel Reisz, The Technique of Film Editing (New York: Farrar, Strauss & Cudahy, 1958), p. 194.

[5]Jay Leyda, Films Beget Films (New York: Hill and Wang, 1964), p. 58.

[6]Ibid.

[7]Burton Benjamin in A. William Bluem, Documentary in American Television (New York: Hastings House, 1965), p. 8.

[8]Richard Byrne, "German Cinematic Expressionism 1919-1924" (unpublished Ph.D. dissertation, State University of Iowa, 1962), p. 313.

[9]Raymond Fielding, "History of the March of Time" (unpublished Masters thesis, UCLA, 1955); Robert Snyder, "A History of the Early Productions of Pare Lorentz and the United States Film Service" (unpublished Ph.D. dissertation, University of Iowa, 1965); Richard Sanderson, "A Historical Study of the Development of American Motion Picture Content and Techniques Prior to 1904" (unpublished Ph.D. dissertation, University of Southern California, 1961).

[10]Donald Fernow, "The Treatment of Social Problems in the Entertainment Film" (unpublished Masters thesis, University of Southern California, 1953); John Kuiper, "Pictorial Composition in the Cinema" (unpublished Masters thesis, State University of Iowa, 1957); James Sieger, "An Analysis of Catholic-Censorship of Motion Picture Films in the United States" (unpublished Masters thesis, University of Southern California, 1957).

[11]Charles Palmer, "The Use of Sound Motion Pictures in the Measurement of Speech Skills" (unpublished Ph.D. dissertation, University of Wisconsin, 1955); Hoyt Griffith, "An Experimental Investigation to Determine the Instructional and Persuasive Effects of Film Music in an Educational Film" (unpublished Masters thesis, University of Southern California, 1958).

[12] Theodore Terry, "The Negro in Hollywood: A Critical Study of Entertainment Films Containing Negro Themes" (unpublished Masters thesis, University of Southern California, 1962); Joseph Richen, "An Analysis of Four Screenplays of Ingmar Bergman" (unpublished Masters thesis, Ohio University, 1962); Robert Kantor, "A Critical Survey of the Use of Creative Sound in Motion Pictures" (unpublished Masters thesis, University of Southern California, 1957).

[13] Charles Pillow, "Survey of Documentary and Technical Cine Photography at the Air Force Flight Test Center" (unpublished Masters thesis, University of Southern California, 1965); Peter Drowne, "An Investigation into the Evolution of Motion Picture Photography and Film Usage in the United States Marine Corps" (unpublished Masters thesis, University of Southern California, 1957); Ross Vincent, "Historical Study of the Army Air Forces First Motion Picture Unit (18th AAFEC) in World War II" (unpublished Masters thesis, University of Southern California, 1959); Merle Lewey, "Historical and Operational Record Films in the Department of the Army" (unpublished Masters thesis, University of Southern California, 1959); Paul Myatt, "A Survey of the Use of Motion Pictures in Flight Training by the United States Navy (unpublished Masters thesis, University of Southern California, 1957); Richard MacCann, "Documentary Film and Democratic Government: An Administrative History from Pare Lorentz to John Huston" (unpublished Ph.D. dissertation, Harvard, 1951).

[14] W. Hugh Baddeley, The Technique of Documentary Film Production (New York: Hastings House, 1963), p. 9.

[15] Lewis Herman, Educational Films (New York: Crown Publishers, Inc., 1965), p. 6.

[16] Richard MacCann, "Documentary Film and Democratic Government: An Administrative History from Pare Lorentz to John Huston" (unpublished Ph.D. dissertation, Harvard, 1951), p. 80.

[17] Gloria Waldron, The Information Film (New York: Columbia University Press, 1949), p. 24.

[18] Quoted in Bluem, p. 33.

[19] Waldron, p. 22.

[20] Marion Sheridan, Harold Owen, Ken Macrorie, and Fred Marcus, The Motion Picture and the Teaching of English (New York: Appleton-Century-Crofts, 1965), p. 113.

[21] Waldron, p. 17.

[22]Robert and Nancy Katz, "Documentary in Transition, Part II: The International Scene and the American Documentary," *Quarterly of Radio-Television-Film*, IV (1949-50), 52.

[23]Baddeley, p. 9.

[24]Roy Stryker quoted in Bluem, pp. 24-25.

[25]MacCann, p. 80.

[26]Rotha, Road and Griffith, p. 115.

[27]John Grierson, "Dramatizing Housing Needs and City Planning," *Films*, I (November, 1939), p. 86.

[28]Sheridan, Owen, Macrorie and Marcus, p. 113.

[29]Bluem, p. 42.

[30]Rotha, Road and Griffith, p. 117.

[31]John Grierson quoted in Arthur Knight, *The Liveliest Art* (New York: The Macmillan Company, 1957), p. 211.

[32]Rotha, Road and Griffith, p. 116.

[33]*Ibid.*, p. 101.

[34]Bluem, p. 13.

[35]Waldron, p. 26.

[36]*Ibid.*

[37]Cecile Starr, *Ideas on Film* (New York: Funk and Wagnalls Co., 1951), p. 53.

[38]Grierson quoted in Rotha, Road and Griffith, p. 43.

[39]*Ibid.*, p. 114.

[40]Irving Jacoby in Starr, p. xiii.

[41]Baddeley, p. 9.

[42]Bluem, p. 15.

[43]Rotha, Road and Griffith, pp. 31-32.

[44]*Ibid.*, p. 115.

[45]John Grierson in the preface to Paul Rotha, Documentary Film (London: Faber & Faber, Ltd., 1936), p. 5.

[46]Rotha, Road and Griffith, p. 358.

[47]Ibid., p. 75.

[48]Starr, p. xiv.

[49]Rotha, Road and Griffith, p. 268.

[50]Ibid., p. 278.

[51]Ibid., p. 276.

[52]Ibid., p. 334.

[53]Ibid., p. 200.

[54]Rotha and Griffith, p. 459.

[55]Arthur L. Mayer, "Fact into Film," Public Opinion Quarterly, VIII (Summer, 1944), 210.

[56]Rotha, Road and Griffith, pp. 315-329.

[57]Rotha and Griffith, p. 459.

[58]Ibid.

[59]Richard Byrne, "Stylistic Analysis of the Film: Notes on a Methodology," Speech Monographs, XXX (March, 1965), 74-78.

[60]John Kuiper, "An Analysis of the Four Silent Films of Sergei Mikhailovich/Eisenstein" (unpublished Ph.D. dissertation, University of Iowa, 1960), p. 18.

CHAPTER II

THE DOCUMENTARY FILM IN WAR

This chapter is a review and history of the documentary film in
war. It covers both the military and civilian use in World War I and
World War II. The context and style of the films in war were not
different from those in peace. It was the sheer volume of production
and degree of excellence achieved by so many films that makes this
chapter necessary. As Richard Griffith stated, "It was World War II
. . . that was responsible for the great growth in the production and
use of idea films in America."[1] In both civilian and military quarters,
films for purposes of education, information and persuasion were seen
by more people than ever before or since. At the Army's peak, there
was a nightly audience of more than 1,900,000 men.[2] In 1943, more
than 8,500,000 workers a month saw industrial incentive films in over
135,000 war plants.[3]

WORLD WAR I

Despite their tremendous growth and use in World War II, motion
pictures for information and persuasion were not original with this
conflict. Documentary films, although not labeled as such, were used
extensively during the First World War to stimulate civilian morale,
to inform people overseas about the American way of life and to train
and indoctrinate military personnel.

The use of the photographic medium to portray the image of war has its roots as far back as the Civil War. The forerunner of all combat photographers was Mathew D. Brady, whose documentation of the Civil War was the initial step in the use of the camera to record the patterns of war. By 1865, Brady and his assistants had compiled a collection of over 7,500 photographs.[4] On the Confederate side, A. D. Lytle took photographs of Union forces and then, at the risk of being shot as a spy, smuggled them back to Confederate lines.[5] During the Spanish-American war, various Signal Corps Companies of the Army in Cuba and the Phillipines were issued photographic equipment, resulting in numerous photographs.[6]

With the advent of World War I, the motion picture and war met for the first time. As George Creel stated: "At the very outset, it was obvious that the motion picture had to be placed on the same plane of importance as the written and spoken word."[7] Both domestically and overseas, the motion picture for the first time portrayed the reality of war.

Civilian

The first real juncture of the screen and war came through the Red Cross which started a bureau of pictures. These films were not theatrical pictures, however. They lacked "punch" and, consequently, reached a small audience.[8]

The Committee of Public Information

The civilian use of documentary film in World War I was essentially the story of the Committee of Public Information. On April 14,

1917, George Creel was appointed chairman of the newly created Committee of Public Information. His job was to be both a censor and a press agent for the war.[9] The title of the book describing his work and experiences, How We Advertised America, sets forth the essential function of the CPI. One important facet of this campaign was the motion picture. The CPI was immediately recognized by the War Department as the one authorized organization for the distribution of Signal Corps motion pictures. In this respect the CPI functioned much as did the Office of War Information in World War II.

Initially, the CPI sought to avoid competition with commercial producers. Thus, the bulk of the material received from the War Department was distributed at a nominal price among the newsreel companies. Experts were then engaged to put the remaining footage into feature films. These were handed over to State Councils of Defense and other patriotic societies. The features were shown in theaters, but no admission was charged.[10]

However, the system proved expensive and it failed to show America's progress in the war to large groups of people. As Creel stated: "The growth of the Signal Corps great Photographic Section was producing an enormous amount of material, both in the United States and France, possessed of the very highest propaganda value, and the existing arrangement wasted what it did not fritter away."[11]

Thus, on March, 1918, the civilian pictorial activities of the war were turned over to Creel, who in turn created the Division of Pictures of the CPI with Charles S. Hart as head.

Hart immediately set about trying to connect the flow of war
pictures available from the Signal Corps and other sources to the
established channel of distribution--the motion picture industry.
This procedure met with resistance from the free and profit oriented
industry. As a consequence, Hart and the CPI were forced into the
motion picture business. As Creel commented, "In plain, the Committee
of Public Information went into the motion-picture business as a producer and exhibitor."[12]

Features. The most important films produced by the CPI were
three seven-reel features: (1) Pershing's Crusaders, (2) America's
Answer, (3) Under Four Flags. These films were exhibited initially by
the CPI itself in large cities to establish value and create demand.
Then they were contracted on a percentage basis for subsequent circulation through distributors. George Bowles, the "exploiter" of Birth of
a Nation, was in charge of distribution. He had as many as eight road
companies in different sections of the country at one time, each with
its own advertising, advance sales and business manager.[13]

Utmost care was taken with the "official showings" to exhibit an
impressiveness that would lift the films out of the ordinary motion
picture class. The CPI consulted experts on scenic details, orchestra-
tion and similar special effects. Marcus Beeman conducted an extensive
publicity campaign of two weeks for each film.[14] Each showing lasted
over a week. The three films were officially shown in over sixty-five
cities.[15] Pershing's Crusaders and America's Answer played over 4,000
theater bookings apiece with film rentals for each totaling $180,000.
Under Four Flags had 1,800 bookings with over $60,000 in rentals.[16]

The Allied War Review. However, features alone did not consume all the material received from the Signal Corps. Consequently, the CPI decided to produce a weekly release. Partnerships were entered into with England, France and Italy. Each of these countries along with the United States contributed one-fourth of the material and shared in the profits. The product was called "The Allied War Review."[17] It was edited by Charles Urban and Ray Hall, the first editors of Hearst newsreels.[18] Pathe Exchange was awarded the distribution contract. Eighty percent of the proceeds went to the CPI with a guarantee of showing in 25,000 theaters minimum.[19] The "Review" had almost 6,000 bookings with over \$334,000 in rentals.[20] Total receipts of the Division of Films amounted to \$850,000 with circulation reaching about one-third of the total available people in the United States.[21]

Scenario Department. The CPI was still not satisfied with the motion pictures' contribution to the war effort. Thus, in June, 1918, the Division of Films formed a Scenario Department. The CPI contracted commercially with four producers to make a series of one-reel pictures. The Division of Films supplied the scenarios, a list of locations and permits for filming. They also gave cooperation without charge. The finished picture became the sole property of the producer who obligated himself to the widest possible circulation. Rufus Steele was in charge of this arrangement by which eighteen one-reel films, one six- and one eight-reel film were made.[22]

Late in the summer of 1918, the CPI decided to undertake further productions completing six two-reelers, with an additional six set up when the Armistice came.[23]

The entire output of the Division of Films was made available to the Foreign Section of the CPI for circulation in the various allied countries. The Educational Department also furnished CPI pictures free to organizations throughout the United States. Films were also loaned to the Army and Navy.[24]

The CPI was abolished by congressional enactment on June 30, 1919. With it went the United States government's first large-scale effort to make documentary films. George Creel, in somewhat overzealous tones, described the endeavor:

> A steady output, ranging from one-reel subjects to seven-reel features, and covering every detail of American life, endeavor, and purpose, carried the call of the country to every community in the land, and then, captioned in all the various languages, went over the seas to inform and enthuse the peoples of Allied and neutral nations.[25]

Objective critical assessment of the films in terms of style and technique is virtually nonexistent, as are prints of the films themselves. They were "flagwaving" and propagandistic in purpose, to be sure. However, being "compiled" from Signal Corps' footage, they were essentially realistic in concept. Beyond this, little can be said. Terry Ramsaye, noted film historian and critic, may have summed up their critical value when he stated, "The peculiar fact for screen history is that the vast experience of the war contributed nothing whatever to the art of the motion picture."[26]

Military

While the civilian effort in war films contributed little to the art of the motion picture, it might also be said from the very lack of material written that the military use of film during World War I was even less significant. Historians are not even clear as to when the Army--the Signal Corps in particular--began to use motion pictures for training and education. One of the first known instances of their use was in 1909, when an official test flight by the Wright Brothers was recorded.[27] Several Army films such as U.S. Army Maneuvers, Ft. Leavenworth, Kansas (1909), and American Field Artillery Maneuvers (1911), among others, followed this initial venture. The first U.S. Army training film, Close Order Drill, was produced in 1916.[28]

With the United States' entry into World War I, the need for training films became even more urgent. J. D. Bray, a pioneer in educational films, produced a sample set of training films for the Army at his own expense in 1917. On the basis of this demonstration, the Army decided to move ahead with an expanded program, Bray being commissioned to make a majority of the films.[29]

A Captain Ellis of the 17th Infantry was detached to take charge of the program. In August, 1917, a Photographic Division composed of five officers was set up in the Office of the Chief Signal Officer. Three training schools were established and by the end of the war the Division consisted of fifty-four photographic officers and 418 enlisted men.[30]

During World War I contracts were drawn for sixty-two training films made by commercial producers under Signal Corps' supervision. These films remained in circulation until 1928.[31] In addition, the General Staff was charged with maintaining a history of the war. The Signal Corps also furnished the footage for the CPI films and newsreels.

POST WORLD WAR I

Following the war, the photographic activities of the Signal
Corps were drastically curtailed in keeping with the general de-
escalation of the armed services. In 1925, however, the publicity
activity of the Army was given to the Signal Corps. This resulted in
the creation of the Signal Corps Pictorial Service. It offered current
and World War I coverage to newsreels. In October, 1929, the Signal
Corps was charged with all photographic and cinematic work by the Army.
To meet this charge the Signal Corps established and maintained a
photographic laboratory in Washington, D.C.[32]

Experimentation continued throughout the 1920's and 1930's,
although production was understandably limited. Between the end of
World War I and 1940 approximately two hundred reels were produced by
the Army.[33] The Signal Corps began experimenting with sound in 1928
and by 1933 was producing sound films, although 16mm sound films and
projectors were not in use in service commands until 1936.[34]

PRE-WORLD WAR II BUILDUP

Military

In 1937, the Signal Corps Laboratory at the Army War College in
Washington, D.C., maintained a complete motion picture production unit
which made approximately six subjects a year.[35] This quota was obviously
not enough. In response to a continuing demand for training films, the
War Department, in 1937, set a yearly production rate of twenty films.
Although this number was modest by soon-to-be realized standards, the
Signal Corps had not produced this many in the last ten years. In
order to meet this demand, Major Melvin Gillette, director of the

Signal Corps Photo Lab, organized and headed up a Training Film Field Unit in June, 1937.[36]

In May, 1938, Captain R. T. Schlosberg, the officer in charge of the Photographic Division of the Signal Corps, prepared an article expressing the Army's philosophy toward the use of film. He stated:

> Training films are of outstanding value as a substitute for the physical demonstration of equipment and technique. . . . Of equal or greater importance is their habitual use for orientation purposes . . . ."[37]

The original order charging the Signal Corps with all photographic responsibility was revised in 1939 to make the Chief Signal Officer in charge. Responsibility for all training films was added to this in March, 1940.[38] By November, 1940, a large civilian army created by the peacetime draft was assembled and the need for more training films became acute. The Signal Corps increased its production of film from an average of forty reels a year in 1936 to over 3,000 by 1941.[39]

Civilian

At the same time a military expansion in film activity was occurring, the Federal Government--particularly certain reform agencies-- became very conscious of the possibilities of the documentary film in communicating social messages. The Office of Education, for example, began producing industrial training films; and the U.S. Public Health Service produced at least ten pictures on a variety of health subjects.[40] The most ambitious and noteworthy project was the Resettlement Administration's "commissioning" of Pare Lorentz to produce a film, The Plow That Broke the Plains. For the next five years several government agencies and various private organizations sponsored numerous documentary films. This activity culminated in the formation of the

U.S. Film Service in 1938, headed by Lorentz.[41]

The same year saw the formation of the first in a line of govern-

ment film-making agencies culminating in the formation of the Office

of War Information in 1942. The Office of Government Reports was the

first such agency in 1939, with Lowell Mellet as chief. The Division

of Information in the Office of Emergency Management was dated from a

Presidential letter to Wayne Coy in February, 1941. The Coordinator

of Information was organized in July, 1941, with Robert Sherwood as

head of its Foreign Information section. The last agency was the

Office of Facts and Figures established by executive order in October,

1941, with Archibald Macleish as director.[42] All of this government

film activity, although looked upon with great suspicion by propaganda-

conscious congressmen, prepared the United States for the film demands

of World War II.

WORLD WAR II

Civilian

The aforementioned agencies made many films up to and after

December 7, 1941. However, after Pearl Harbor, lack of coordination

and an increase in competition became the dominant elements in govern-

ment film production. This clearly was not serving the government's

purpose in informing and persuading the American people.

Office of War Information

In June, 1942, President Roosevelt issued Executive Order 9182

creating the Office of War Information.[43] The OWI was composed of the

previously existing OFF, OGR, the Division of Information of OEM and
the Foreign Information Section of the COI. The directive setting up
the bureau stated:

> The OWI will serve as the central point of contact
> between the motion picture industry, theatrical and
> non-theatrical, and . . . will produce motion pictures
> and will review and approve all proposals for the pro-
> duction and distribution of motion pictures by Federal
> Departments and agencies.[44]

Bureau of Motion Pictures. Film activity of the OWI centered in
the Bureau of Motion Pictures which included both a Domestic and Overseas Branch. Lowell Mellet, Head of OGR and Coordinator of Government
Films, was named Chief, with Arch Mercey as his assistant.

Domestic Branch. The Domestic Branch of the Film Bureau consisted
of five divisions: (1) Office of the Chief, (2) Nontheatrical Division,
(3) Coordination Division, (4) Newsreel Division, (5) Production Division. The activities of the Bureau were essentially three-fold. It
was first of all responsible for the creation and production of war
films. Secondly, it was to coordinate the motion picture activities
of other government agencies. Finally, it acted as a liaison with the
motion picture industry in order to obtain the greatest possible distribution of government war films and to assist the industry in making
its own films significant to the prosecution of the war.[45]

The production story of the OWI is brief. It produced four types
of films. The first were feature-length productions. The most applauded
and well-received was Sam Spewak's World at War, a compilation film similar to Capra's Prelude to War for the "Why We Fight" series. The second
type of film was the "short subject" release. These one- and two-reel
films dealt with such national issues and problems as Salvage, Fuel

Conservation, Japanese Relocation and Colleges at War. A total of
seventy-three short subjects were supplied to exhibitors.[46] The third
type of film released by the OWI was the "regional special." These
films emphasized a specific aspect of the war, such as Women Wanted or
Get a War Job. They were usually designed for a particular area of the
country. The fourth type of film produced was footage of factual war
information prepared by the Motion Picture Bureau for use by newsreel
companies.

The OWI also acted as a distributor for other government agency
films, Hollywood-produced war films, and films of the armed forces, including the "Why We Fight" series. As Richard MacCann noted:

> The pattern of OWI's campaign was not greatly
> different from the Film Division of the CPI, at
> least not in the amount of films produced. The
> big difference was in tone and taste.[47]

There was as much, if not more, emphasis on information and persuasion.
However, the form of persuasion was seemingly more objective, relying
more on acceptance of facts objectively presented than the frank emotional appeals so common to World War I films. Patriotism was still
present in World War II films. Unlike World War I films, it was not
worn on one's sleeve.

In 1942-43, the Bureau employed 142 persons with over sixty in
production. The budget for this fiscal year was $1,346,405.[48] However,
this film-making activity was to be short-lived. In 1943, Congress,
ever suspicious of a government propaganda agency and "actuated probably
more by antagonism to the Administration than affection for economy,"
cut OWI's budget from seven million to two million with $50,000 allo-
cated to the Motion Picture Bureau to "carry on liaison activities

between the Government and the film industry."[49] This was the end of

OWI film production. The function was taken over by the Hollywood War

Activities Committee. As Elmer Davis, head of OWI, stated:

> The Domestic Branch of the OWI was a cocktail shaken
> up out of three very dissimilar ingredients--pre-
> decessor organizations which differed widely in their
> objective as well as their techniques. It took almost
> a year, until June, 1943, to create a blend that was
> reasonably satisfactory to the executives of the agency;
> and about the time that this was accomplished, Congress
> poured most of the contents of the shaker down the drain.[50]

War Activities Committee

As early as 1940, Hollywood became concerned with the government's

increasing use of film and the growing threat of war to which they felt

they ought to respond. Film News stated in 1940 that the motion picture

industry was about to announce the appointment of a special representa-

tive committee to cooperate with the defense set up. "Thus, after

several weeks of milling around, Washington and Hollywood appear to

have made complete contact."[51] The result of this contact was the

formation of the Hollywood War Activities Committee in 1940. The WAC

was composed of the leading executives of all branches of the motion

picture industry. Its coordinating committee, headed by George Schaefer,

represented various divisions of the industry, including producers, dis-

tributors, newsreels, the trade press, publicity and advertising and

theaters. The executive staff was headed by Vice-Chairman Francis

Harmon of the Hays Office.[52]

The job of the WAC, at first--before the birth and subsequent

death of the OWI--was the preparation and distribution of documentary

and newsreel films in collaboration with the Coordinator of Government

Films, Lowell Mellet. Outstanding among the films produced by the WAC
at this time was the "America Speaks" series, including such films as
Mr. Blabbermouth, Letter from Bataan, We Refuse to Die and Everybody's
War.[53] When the OWI began producing films, WAC acted as the distribution agency for them. If the films were accepted, prints were made
and supplied to one of the major companies for distribution. The
facilities of the 16,000 theaters represented by the theater owners
and exhibitors in the WAC were pledged for the exhibition of war
information films without charge.[54] When the production of information
shorts by the OWI was discontinued, the WAC stepped into the breach.
It supplied annually without charge fifty-two messages compiled by the
OWI from various government agencies. Twenty-six of these were shorts
of approximately one thousand feet and twenty-six were bulletins con-
sisting of brief messages attached to newsreels.[55] Despite major
Hollywood stars' being commissioned for these commentaries, general
critical consensus felt the films were not of outstanding merit. The
reason for this was essentially because the men who were the backbone
of the documentary movement--Lorentz, Ivens, Van Dyke and others--were
making documentaries for the armed forces. Most of the WAC-produced
films were, as a result, dull and uninspiring, especially when they
followed Betty Grable or Dorothy Lamour.

This did not apply to all industry information films, however.
"The March of Time" continued its prewar pattern of presenting timely,
interesting issues in a fast-moving, visually stimulating format. RKO's
"This is America" series, a monthly two-reeler treating such themes as
V-Mail, was equally well made and received. However, these were the

exceptions. Despite the patriotic stand taken by the exhibitors and
theater owners to exhibit war films, World War II film activity was
marked by a constant battle between industry and government over their
exhibition. Fuel for the exhibitors' argument that the public didn't
want this material was that even such outstanding documentary features
as Prelude to War and The Battle of Russia did poorly.

Far more popular than the historical compilation film or information short were the well-timed releases direct from the battle-fronts,
such as the British film Desert Victory, Zanuck's Report from the
Aleutians and John Ford's The Battle of Midway.

In connection with these up-to-date releases were the ever-present
newsreels. Although not documentary in the strict sense of the word,
they did present reality in a dramatic way. The drama exuded more
from the actual content itself, however, than from any particular cinematic construction. The newsreels, as in the past, were essentially a
compilation of weekly headlines and short stories told objectively and
straightforwardly. Approximately thirty-fifty percent of any newsreel
was composed of Signal Corps footage.[56]

A final but important aspect of domestic war time information
films was the films produced for civilian defense and the distribution
of films made by various agencies, both military and civilian. The
Office of Civilian Defense, for example, produced films beginning in
1942. They continued to produce about ten films a year throughout the
war. The films were used as springboards in training sessions for
civilian defense training classes as well as for the information of
local councils and civic groups.[57]

The OWI distribution system of 16mm films was impressive. Virtually all of the films produced or approved by the OWI went not only into theaters, but were shown to schools, civic groups, and American Legion posts through an elaborate distribution system. The viewing audience was not restricted to those people who had the time or the money to go to theaters. The films, rather, reached into every available community and group with their message.

Although it actually produced films for just over one year, the OWI achieved remarkable coverage for its films. Through its efforts, even after its budget was slashed, the facts and information of the war were made available to the American people as never before. Taken as a whole, however, and in comparison to the military effort, the domestic civilian motion picture role in World War II was relatively minor and achieved limited results.

Military

The case for the military is much more positive. Throughout World War II, War Department film production and distribution costs were over $50,000,000 annually.[58] The library of uncut war film compiled by the armed forces totaled 13 1/2 million feet.[59] It was estimated that over 10,500,000 hours of soldier time were spent each month seeing War Department films.[60] Thus, from a purely physical standpoint the military use of the information film in World War II surpassed anything known before or since. However, it was also the technique, results and functions of the films that made the military film program more important and vital than any film program in the history of the motion picture.

Signal Corps Organization

The responsibility for military film, outside of the Air Force and the Navy, which had their own film organizations, fell upon the Signal Corps. As was outlined earlier, the Signal Corps photographic activities dated back to the Spanish-American War. The film activity of the Signal Corps increased tremendously during World War I, tailed off during the postwar period and with war again imminent, mushroomed into tremendous activity. The organization, history and development of the Signal Corps film activity in World War II is the subject of separate research itself. To provide clearer background for the military use of film in World War II, and specifically the place of the "Why We Fight" series in the setup, a brief outline is necessary.

In 1924, Photographic Services was a branch under the Signal Corps Intelligence Division (one of five divisions).[61] By 1934, the Signal Corps had seven divisions including photography.[62] By July, 1941, the Signal Corps had increased to eleven divisions.[63] Photography was by this time unofficially divided into two branches, motion pictures and still pictures. With the United States entry into World War II, the Signal Corps photographic responsibility grew tremendously. Thus, the Photographic Division was raised to the level of a "service"; designated the Army Pictorial Service on June 17, 1942.[64] APS was tossed around for a year or so, first dropping "back down" to division status, then being removed from Signal Corps jurisdiction. However, by May, 1943, the APS was re-established as a service and returned to the Signal Corps. It remained there for the duration of the war.

Despite the activity during World War I and after, the military value of photography was not fully recognized in the pre-World War II years. It was still considered a luxury by many--nice enough if it could be arranged, but of little military value. This concept changed rapidly in the so-called "emergency period" following the start of war in Europe in 1939. Army training officers were suddenly confronted with the problem of converting thousands of draftees into an Army. Soon every part of the Army became a sellers' market for photography. Wherever civilians were being transformed into soldiers, the Army wanted training films in quantity. To meet this demand, the Signal Corps expanded both its training and production program. In 1936, the War Department scheduled production of twenty films a year.[65] In 1941, the program involved 192 subjects alone, any one of which might require as many as five training films.[66]

The crowded conditions at the two training film production centers at Fort Monmouth and Wright Field, coupled with obstacles created by early draft procedures, held training and production below their desired point. The Signal Corps, in an effort to relieve the situation, began to put plans into effect to use the resources of Hollywood. In 1940, the industry accepted sponsorship of certain photographic units under the Affiliated Plan. In the same year planning for Hollywood production of training films got under way. The large studios notified the Secretary of War that they would produce the films at cost.[67] The coordinating agency for these activities was the Research Council of the Academy of Motion Picture Arts and Sciences. The work began immediately without financial arrangements completely

firm. However, speed was more important than economy. If the masses
of men entering the Army were to be trained, they would have to take a
major part of their instruction from films. Four basic pictures, Sex
Hygiene, Personal Hygiene, The Articles of War and Military Courtesy
and Customs of the Service were in demand for all reception centers.
It was a fruit of the arrangement with the Research Council that the
Signal Corps was able to distribute these within the first six months
of the draft, the first two being ready by March, 1941.[68]

In connection with this work, Darryl Zanuck, head of the Research
Council of the Academy of Arts and Sciences, undertook a study, at
Chief of Staff Marshall's prodding, to evaluate the training film program in the Army. He reported that there was a "complete absence of
coordination between the production, distribution and use of training
films."[69] He stated that the Army should either drop its film training
program altogether or standardize and run it according to the methods
of the motion picture industry.[70] There were advocates of both alterna-
tives. Fortunately, Colonel E. M. Gillette prevailed with his proposal
for the "liberation of the Signal Corps training film program from the
benevolent despotism of the Motion Picture Academy's Research Council."[71]

Pearl Harbor brought an abrupt close to the debate concerning
Signal Corps responsibility for films. It also ended the debate over
whether the Signal Corps should purchase the Paramount Studios at
Astoria, Long Island. In February, 1942, the plant was activated as
the Signal Corps Photographic Center. After extensive remodeling, it
opened in May, 1942, with Colonel Gillette in command.[72] Thus, after

six months of war, the Signal Corps had an up-to-date plant for producing films and training photographic technicians.

All Army motion pictures during World War II, for whatever purpose, were produced either by the Signal Corps itself or by Hollywood under commercial contracts. When the Signal Corps--specifically the Army Pictorial Service--received a request from a government agency or branch of the service to produce a film, the Corps produced a script. After approval by the requesting agency, the Signal Corps decided whether it could make the film in its own studios or whether commercial production was needed. Scripts to be produced commercially went to the Western Division of the SCPC, which analyzed the production problems involved and requested the studio best able to undertake production to begin. Almost without exception, the Hollywood studios produced the films at cost.[73]

Army Pictorial Service. The APS was set up in 1942 as the photographic agency for the Signal Corps. Its mission, after weathering a congressional investigation early in 1943 with no ill effects, remained essentially unchanged during the last two years of the war, although the volume of work nearly doubled. Its work fell into nine divisions. It first of all produced and procured training films, film bulletins and film strips, including foreign language versions. It also produced informational and historical films for military planning and analysis to document campaigns. A third division involved morale and orientation films. APS also procured, but did not produce, entertainment films. It produced hundreds of thousands of still photographs, processed V-mail and operated the world's largest film distributing organization. APS also conducted extensive research. Finally, it trained technicians for all Army photo units except the Army Air Force.[74]

As wartime staff divisions went, the APS staff was relatively small. APS activities centered around the Signal Corps Photographic Center at Astoria, Long Island. About 2,000 military and civilian personnel including writers, producers, cameramen, etc., were employed there. At its peak of operation the SCPC employed 287 officers, 610 enlisted men and 1,361 civilians, housed in fourteen buildings. Also included was the Western Division of the SCPC in Beverly Hills, California.[75]

Another field agency, the Signal Corps Photo Lab, was located at the Army War College in Washington, D.C. It processed all motion picture footage, completed filmstrips and made all portraits and identification photographs.[76]

The APS distributed the Army's films to troops everywhere through a system of film libraries. At the war's peak it was the largest in the world. Overseas Motion Picture Service, through its twenty-one agencies, distributed more entertainment films in one year than the four largest Hollywood producers combined.[77] Films serving different purposes were distributed by different methods. Entertainment pictures and recurring subjects such as the "Army-Navy Screen Magazine" required circulating in order to reach as many troops as possible in the short-est time. Training films, orientation films and other special purpose films were placed in film libraries at specific training installations in order to be on hand immediately.[78]

In summary, the APS and the SCPC could be thought of as a manufacturing plant, turning out one specific product--motion pictures--
in a variety of forms for a fairly large group of diverse customers.
The customers supplied the specifications and the Signal Corps designed,
engineered and produced the specific item desired. Thus, for example,
when the War Department's Bureau of Public Relations decided upon a
film for war workers, it submitted the idea to the Signal Corps which,
in turn, wrote the script and produced the film. In other words,
regardless of the idea or what department submitted it, the interpretation and presentation of the basic film story was in general a Signal
Corps responsibility.

Objectives of Military Films

Motion pictures were used by the Army tô accomplish four basic
objectives:

1) Orientation in the moral purpose for which the war was
   fought, the nature of our allies and our enemies, and
   the importance of the part played by various components
   of the Army.

2) Understanding of the habituation in self-control and
   proper conduct of the individual soldier.

3) Information on current material development and military
   progress on all fronts.

4) Instruction in basic technical subjects and skills.[79]

Types of Military Films

Within these basic objectives several specific forms and styles
of film emerged.

Training Films. The first and most widely used form of film was
the training film; the "nuts and bolts" approach to film instruction.

Much of the early history and organization of training film production
has been previously described, including the association with Hollywood
before the war, the tremendous buildup prior to and after Pearl Harbor,
the creation of the SCPC at Astoria, Long Island, and the organization
and distribution of all Army films, including training films, throughout
the war. However, some detailed information seems necessary to place
this form of information film in proper perspective.

The most numerous, and by some standards the most important,
films produced by the Army during World War II were training films.
In the broad sense of the word, almost every film made by the Army
could be called a training film. The training film in its narrower
concept, however, was a film presenting a part of the established
curriculum of a service school. Throughout the course of the war,
including adaptations and rescoring of certain films into foreign
languages, APS produced more than 2,500 training films.[80] For the
fiscal year 1943, over $10,000,000 was appropriated for training films.[81]
During the same year approximately 135,000 16mm prints and 24,000 35mm
prints of training films were sent to an estimated 320 film libraries
in the United States and overseas. There were 200,000 bookings of
forty-four subjects filmed for the Corps of Engineers alone.[82]

The first training films issued prior to and during the early
months of the war were pretty sorry. Based essentially on a lecture
concept, the films were boring, full of hard-to-relate information and
ineffective. However, after the SCPC was established at Astoria and a
training program for writers, editors, cameramen and producers was
initiated, the training film took on new dimensions. The films soon

began to utilize animation and music, with dialogue written in "G.I. style." Intensive studies were conducted concerning the effectiveness and acceptability of the films. The results showed that throughout the war training films cut training time by at least thirty percent.[83]

The actual production of a training film was always the result of a request from some arm of service. It decided what part of its curriculum it wanted filmed and prepared a picture plan or general outline of the material to be presented. This plan, when approved by the chief of the appropriate service, was the basis for the scenario, prepared either by the Signal Corps or the service itself. The APS with the OFCSO would determine whether the film could be produced at the SCPC or by Hollywood. When the finished film was approved and accepted by the requesting service, the Signal Corps distributed it as instructed by the service.[84]

The number of training films needed during the initial phase of troop buildup early in the war was tremendous. It might have been expected that after the peak of Army mobilization passed, fewer training films would be needed. This was not the case. As the need for films depicting basic training courses declined, new film requirements increased with the steady influx of new weapons pouring from laboratories and production lines. Radar, for example, was a new weapon. The APS hurried into production a series of three films on radar jamming methods, followed by three more on the micro-wave gun-lazer radar SCR-584, finally followed by three more on the general uses of radar.[85]

Dull subjects were transformed into appealing, interesting and informative films. A Quartermaster Corps training film entitled

Conservation of Clothing and Equipage was "a hit" when Robert Ripley
of Believe It or Not fame was obtained to expound the marvels of GI
equipment through statistics.[86]

Films were also produced quickly to meet urgent combat needs.
An example of this was Trench Foot, a film rushed to completion in a
record six weeks.[87] Other timely film bulletins included DDT--Weapon
Against Disease, Diary of a Sergeant and Swing into Step, the story of
the rehabilitation of men who had lost their legs.[88]

When American equipment began flowing into Allied countries, it
became necessary to translate many films into several languages. This
need became so great that the APS set up a Foreign Language Division
in SCPC to handle the work. Four language programs--French, Italian,
Chinese and Latin American--were inaugurated for training films. A
total of 988 films were rescored into foreign languages.[89]

In addition to the full-fledged training films, other types of
visual training aids, such as film bulletins, combat bulletins, film
strips and film slides, served the Army's training program. A film
bulletin was generally a two-reel film dealing with a single specific
topic. Since timeliness was all-important, film bulletins were produced as silent pictures in order to save the time of writing and recording narration. Training instructors and lecturers added their
original commentary as the film was shown.[90]

The training film in World War II was indeed an important tool.
Photography had such a vital role in troop training that training
officers called it their "secret weapon." The credo of the films was
set forth in a writer's orientation course directive which stated,

"Make it clear, make it logical, make it human, and drive home the necessity of learning now, not when you get into battle."[91] Despite the fact that the use and advantages of the films was continually stressed by the services, it was also pointed out that films "supplement but do not supplant the instructor."[92]

Orientation Films. Orientation or morale-building films were relatively slow to develop in comparison to training films. However, they can, perhaps more than any other type of film produced during World War II, be labeled documentary. The concern for morale and the various programs designed to deal with it are detailed in Chapter III and do not need repetition here. However, the general program needs to be placed in the total World War II film picture.

The films labeled "orientation" were produced by the Signal Corps for the Information and Education Division Army Service Forces to help the individual soldier understand why he was in uniform. The films also defined the enemy for him and acquainted him with his allies.

Orientation films were undertaken early in 1942 by a special motion picture production unit under the command of Frank Capra. Originally placed in the I&E Division ASF, Capra's unit undertook the orientation series of films as its principal task.[93]

The original seven, called the "Why We Fight" series, were generally regarded as the films that contributed most to American understanding of the issues of World War II. They were a required part of every soldier's training and were released to war workers and ultimately to the general public as well.

Capra's group also undertook a second series, the "Know Your Enemy" and "Know Your Ally" series. Three films, one each on Japan, Germany and Britain, were produced. Know Your Ally Britain was so effective from the British point of view that Prime Minister Churchill had it shown in all British theaters.[94]

As the war progressed, the orientation film kept pace. Your Job in Germany was readied especially for the occupation in that area. A similar film, This is the Philippines, prepared the invasion forces with the information they needed.[95]

Perhaps one of the most important and certainly the most secretly produced film of World War II was the orientation film Two Down and One to Go. It detailed the Army's plans for re-deploying men to the Pacific and explained the Army's point system for discharge to both military and civilian personnel. Filmed in the summer of 1944, it received its official title on September 8. By the end of December, 1,363 techni-color prints were distributed to various parts of the world in readiness for Germany's surrender. At exactly 1200 Eastern War Time, May 10, 1945, showings of the film began simultaneously to military units and civilian audiences. Within five days, ninety-five percent of all troops in the zone of the interior had seen the films. Ninety-seven percent of the troops overseas viewed the film within two weeks. Over 800 first-run movie theaters in the United States showed the film to the civilian population. A second film, On to Tokyo, was released two weeks later, reaching almost the entire military audience.[96]

Altogether, Capra's unit produced seventeen feature-length orientation films. This was at the rate of about one every two months, during the approximately three years it was assigned to the work.[97]

Historical-Information Films. Another type of film made during World War II by the Armed Forces was the information or historical feature-length film. These films were photographed by Signal Corps and other combat photographers primarily to document the war. They were shown to troops but received their widest use and popularity in civilian theaters. The first of the War Department's historical record series of feature films was John Huston's Report from the Aleutians. This was the record of the construction of an air base on Adak Island. The film depicted the efforts involved in preparing for the attack on Kiska and Attic Islands and detailed the assault itself. The film was photographed in color by Huston, Ray Scott and four others during the fall and winter of 1942.[98] Another outstanding documentary was William Wyler's Memphis Belle, which detailed in simple fashion the business of war in the air. The Fighting Lady, produced by Louis de Rochemont, depicted life aboard an Essex-class aircraft carrier in the Pacific theater. Still other major films of this type included Huston's The Battle of San Pietro, John Ford's The Battle of Midway and Zanuck's At the Front in North Africa.

Lewis Jacobs stated, "The best of them emerged as screen poems lyrically celebrating the courage of ordinary men and charged with an organized hatred of war and killing."[99] He also commented that the latter quality perhaps accounted for the comparative scarcity of films of this kind. After a few experiences, the War Department grew less anxious to permit independent-minded directors to travel freely through combat zones and film what they saw as they felt it.[100] Nonetheless, the historical features outside of the "Why We Fight" series constitute some of the best examples of documentary film to come out of the war.

Army-Navy Screen Magazine. The suggestion for a special news-reel for soldiers was first put forth by Frank Capra early in 1942. In his memorandum to Chief Signal Officer Osborn, Capra stated that the film should have as its prime objective keeping the troops informed on world events, the war, the home front activity and latest enemy weapons and methods. He also conceived of it as a more personal medium through which specific individuals such as FDR and General Marshall could speak. In addition, the film would be an ideal medium by which combat personnel could tell their experiences to the whole Army.[101]

The product of Capra's idea was the "Army-Navy Screen Magazine." The project was headed by Leonard Spigelgass with Henry Berman as editor and Don Etlinger as chief scriptwriter.[102]

The APS produced the first issue of the bi-weekly newsreel in April, 1943. It included material filmed at random by the Navy, the AAF and the Marine Corps, as well as Army film and commercial features.[103] One striking feature of the magazine was the first and perhaps the most popular cartoon figure of World War II--"Private Snafu." "Snafu" was the prototype of all GIs who invariably do everything wrong, much like Yank magazine's "Sad Sack." "Snafu" struggled through a series of in-credible encounters in all branches of the service, from which he always miraculously escaped. He fell out of airplanes, was shot, stabbed, got malaria and dysentery and cracked up jeeps. However, with all his stumbling and misadventure, he always brought home a clear concise point. As the official Signal Corps history stated: ". . . he served as a teacher, morale builder, comrade-in-arms, and safety valve."[104]

Another popular feature incorporated into the "Magazine" in order to elicit active soldier response was "By Request." This feature utilized specific soldiers' requests on film. For example, men in the Tropics asked for shots of a Chicago blizzard and a soldier in the Aleutians begged for a glimpse of his home town.[105] Paul Rotha feels this type of response to "By Request" indicates how closely men were tied to home and how restricted their interests were to the known, familiar and domestic. He uses this to suggest how little the men had actually been educated or oriented.[106] This may certainly have been the case. Other, more objective, research on specific orientation films and objectives points to some of the same observations. Whatever the "Army-Navy Screen Magazine" did or did not show about men's orientation, it did show that soldiers needed and enjoyed film entertainment. The type of features the "Screen Magazine" employed seemed to meet this need. The popularity of the "Screen Magazine" is perhaps best attested to by the fact that 320 prints were made for each of its seventy releases and that when an order for a twenty percent reduction of the use of film was put into effect, the "Screen Magazine" was specifically exempted.[107] James Agee, writing in The Nation, states that the films were miles ahead of the newsreels. "The time and pace are relaxed and sensible--better than waltzing across little bits of broken mirror which make up the average newsreel or suffering through the riveting-hammer maniacal yammer of a 'March of Time'."[108] One of its best techniques, according to Agee, was the frequent use of a shot introduced and given its pure power without sound, music, explanation or comment.[109]

The "Army-Navy Screen Magazine" was usually twenty minutes long and thus too short to justify running alone. It was, therefore, incorporated into the Morale Services forty-five minute program, "G.I. Movie Weekly." This included commercial releases, sports shorts, and standard newsreels. The "Weekly" existed because of a three-way partnership between the Army Pictorial Service, the Special Service Division and the motion picture industry. The arrangement ensured the soldier a steady diet of his favorite entertainment films. The Army Motion Picture Service, a branch of the Special Services Division, secured the films and APS distributed them.[110]

The "G.I. Movie Weekly" undoubtedly had the largest and most appreciative viewers any film series ever enjoyed. OMPS estimated that at the rate of two shows a week, a minimum of 650,000,000 military personnel attended these Army motion picture showings in overseas theaters during the war.[111]

Industrial Incentive Films. Yet another film series produced by the Signal Corps was the industrial incentive film or "Film Communiques." Produced by the Office of the Under Secretary of War, the series was designed to stimulate war production.

The idea began in 1942 when the Labor Consultant to the Under Secretary of War suggested the preparation of a film which would dramatize the responsibilities the war placed upon "our soldiers of production." Captain Richard Maibaum of the APS prepared a script and served as technical advisor to 20th-Century-Fox during the production of the film. By June, 1942, the film Arm Behind the Army had more than 700 showings to an estimated 1,000,000 war workers throughout the country. It won general commendation, and as a result, the Signal Corps was directed to produce one such film each month.[112]

To accommodate this demand, the APS set up the Special Projects Branch. The films were contracted out on a cost basis to the industry. The Signal Corps dubbed foreign language titles and the OWI distributed prints of the films in Allied and neutral countries.[113]

The films were for the most part created out of combat footage. The subjects ranged from Little Detroit, the story of a truck assembly plant in North Africa, to the Price of Rendova, the filming of the landing of invasion troops, establishment of a beachhead and a Japanese air attack. Generally, the films aimed at keeping the war and its myriad problems before the civilian public; often they were created specifically to overcome some lag in production. As one official stated in reference to The Case of the Tremendous Trifle: "We tried to show the guy who makes a lousy little screw nut that he's part of something big."[114] The films enjoyed great success. In March, 1944, Army industrial films played to over 5,600,000 war workers.[115] At the peak, over 8,500,000 workers a month saw the films in war plants.[116]

Navy Films. The Navy relied heavily on films as teaching aids. Unlike the Army, the Navy was not interested in indoctrination or broad information films. It needed films that showed how to run the machinery of war. Also, unlike the Army, the Navy, despite its large production, was not in the film production business. They farmed out their films to private companies.[117]

All Navy films were the responsibility of the Training Film Section of the Photographic Division of the Bureau of Aeronautics.

The section was set up in August, 1941, with Thomas Orchard, assistant producer of "The March of Time," as head.[118] The Photographic Division had been engaged in film work for many years, but the Navy had not previously made any training films. The film operation grew tremendously. Each major ship in the fleet carried its own camera crew with lab, darkroom and projection room. This work was coordinated by the well-known photographer, Edward Steichen.[119] By 1945, the Training Film and Motion Picture Branch employed over 200 persons in Washington, D.C.[120] In three and one-half years the Navy released 1,100 training films, along with 2,200 slide film productions.[121]

The Marine Corps. The Coast Guard and the Marine Corps also made films within the Navy Photographic Division, although the Marine Corps film activity remained separate. The Marine Corps motion picture work centered in the Marine Corps Photographic Section at Quantico, Virginia. The section was organized in January, 1941, with the first films produced in November, 1941. The section carried out scenario preparation, animation and editing, and exercised supervision over the remaining phases of production under commercial contract.[122]

Army Air Force. Independent Army Air Force motion picture activity began only after a lengthy and sometimes bitter fight with the Army. In 1939, a laboratory was set up at Wright Field to make training films exclusively for the use of the Air Force. With the expansion of the general Army program at Washington and Astoria, the AAF Film Production Lab at Wright Field rapidly grew into an organization resembling a commercial studio. The AAF, however, remained unsatisfied. What it really wanted was control of its own film activities, as General H.

Arnold made clear by his directive of June, 1942.[123] Without waiting
for official approval, the AAF set up the First Motion Picture Unit.
A meeting between Signal Corps and AAF representatives finally resulted
in the AAF handling its own film work. By October, 1942, the AAF was
operating its own film production unit.[124]

Other Film Uses. There were, of course, other military uses of
film during World War II, including secret "Staff Reports," "Combat
Bulletins" and a chronology of the war. However, these film programs
were minor in comparison to the general training and orientation film
programs. They were in some cases highly secret and in others never
completed.

Staff Film Reports. The "Staff Film Report," of all the "minor"
uses of film by the military in World War II, was perhaps the most important. The "Report" consisted of a weekly compilation of the most
pertinent shots of tactical situations embodying use of troops and
equipment. The films were shown to a select group of high-level staff
officers in Washington, D.C. and from all theaters of operation.
According to the Signal Corps official historian, "At high levels the
'Staff Film Reports' were rated as the most valuable of all film
projects APS undertook during the war."[125] Once the restricted
material was eliminated, the "Report" became a "Combat Bulletin" and
was issued to the troops.

Historical Chronology. Throughout the war, the Historical Branch
of the SCPS collected and filed film sequences of all American operations
in the various theaters and campaigns for use at the war's end in com-
piling chronologies. Unfortunately, only a small number were ever

completed. With the sharp postwar reduction in funds and personnel, the program was all but halted in 1946. Only fourteen of a projected fifty-nine films were ever completed.[126]

Foreign and Overseas Documentary

The extensive amount of rescoring and dubbing of films into various languages by the Signal Corps has already been noted. However, some mention should be made of the excellent film work done overseas by the Office of War Information Overseas and the Coordinator of Inter-American Affairs.

CPI Foreign Section

War films for overseas consumption originated with the Committee of Public Information in World War I. As in the United States, motion pictures played a great part in the work of the CPI's Foreign Section. Jules Brulatour was in charge of the program and toured the country collecting "educational stuff" showing what America was like.[127] He went around to various manufacturing concerns that "went in for motion pictures," such as Ford, U.S. Steel, International Harvester, among others. Lt. John Turek, borrowed from the Army, helped Brulatour in duplicating prints and putting motion pictures into other languages in the old Kalem studios on West 23rd Street in New York.[128]

This tradition was carried forth on a much larger scale in World War II by OWI Overseas and the CIAA.

OWI Overseas

The OWI Overseas Branch was headed by Robert Riskin, well-known screenwriter for many Frank Capra films. Assisting him were

Phillip Dunne and Irving Lerner.[129]   At first, OWI Overseas reviewed

the films that were on hand, much in the same fashion as Brulatour's

Foreign Section in World War I.   Out of more than 2,000 documentaries

reviewed, some 500 were selected as providing material suitable for

distribution overseas.   Twenty-five of these were then acquired by OWI

and were rewritten, re-edited and rescored.   They were then released

overseas.   Among the films acquired and released were Power and the

Land, the "Why We Fight" series, Memphis Belle and Tarawa.[130]   OWI

Overseas also issued a weekly newsreel titled "United News" made in

cooperation with the five major newsreel companies in the world.[131]

In addition, several feature-length films surveying the war were pro-

duced.   These were entitled News Review No. 1, News Review No. 2, and

so on.[132]   The Overseas Branch also produced a number of twenty-minute

short subjects collectively called "U.S.A. Screen Magazine."   Each

reel emphasized some phase of American culture, industry and achieve-

ment.   They were issued monthly.[133]

However, the chief film activity of OWI Overseas consisted of

the production of some thirty to forty original documentaries designed

to "project life in the United States."[134]   The most famous of these

was perhaps Arturo Toscannini, with the maestro himself conducting

Verdi's stirring "Hymn to the Nations."   Other films in addition to

this included such topics as Swedes in America, Cowboy, Valley of the

Tennessee and Autobiography of a Jeep.[135]

OWI prepared many of the films in as many as twenty-two languages.

They were distributed through U.S. film companies' foreign subsidiaries

and local civic groups to over seventy countries.[136]   With the exception of the Toscannini movie, the films of the Overseas Branch were produced solely for distribution to civilian audiences overseas and not for domestic use in the United States.[137] This fact, alone, may have been responsible for the Overseas Branch's being able to carry on production when the Domestic Branch was literally "budgeted out of existence." Congress was not averse to "propaganda" being sent overseas. The cry of "New Deal" or "4th Term" propaganda was not heard here as it was surrounding the work of the Domestic Branch.

Coordinator of Inter-American Affairs

The other important element in overseas documentary was the Office of the Coordinator of Inter-American Affairs. The CIAA was established by executive order of the Council of National Defense in August, 1940, with Nelson Rockefeller as head. The CIAA was a war information agency, but mainly through the efforts of Rockefeller, it was kept separate from the OWI.[138]

The Motion Picture Division of the CIAA was set up in October, 1940, with John Jay Whitney and later Francis Alstock as head. Initially, there was no production unit. The CIAA motion picture function consisted essentially of seeing that irritating elements did not crop up in Hollywood films which went to Latin and South America. The CIAA also engineered the agreement on the part of the United States distributors to withdraw all U.S. films from theaters in Latin and South America which showed Axis films. This was a major accomplishment in the information war and had immediate effects, especially in the showing of newsreels.[139]

However, this essentially negative program was altered when Julien Bryan assumed the leadership of the film unit in 1943. Bryan was an independent producer and lecturer, most famous for his journalistic film scoop of the fall of Warsaw.[140] Immediately upon assuming the position, Bryan brought in 100,000 feet of his own film on Latin America. Along with material furnished by "The March of Time," seven titles were quickly released. Bryan then made several trips south and brought back material for many more films.[141] Originally the films were for foreign distribution only, but soon many of the films were being distributed through non-theatrical channels in the United States. One of the best of the CIAA films in this respect was Willard Van Dyke's The Bridge.[142] The films followed no "propaganda line" but dealt primarily with matters of health, agriculture and education. Typical of these films were Montevideo Family, the story of a middle class family in Uruguay, Housing in Chile and Feudal System in Bolivia.[143]

The CIAA films that created the greatest interest and were the best known and remembered are those of Walt Disney. With his cartoon characters, Disney became what the New York Times described as "the country's No. 1 propagandist."[144] Typical of the films produced by Disney was Saludos Amigos, an amiable, rambling travelogue of Donald Duck going through South America. Other more educational subjects included The Winged Scourge, a lesson on malaria, Defense Against Invasion and Maize: Grain that Built the Hemisphere.[145] The most ambitious plan of Disney involved the use of visual aids to eradicate adult illiteracy in the Latin American republics. The program which Disney, himself, described as being "fightening in scope" included

the production of twenty-seven subjects where cartoon characters
Donald Duck, Mickey Mouse and others taught reading, writing and arith-
metic in Spanish, Portuguese and English.[146] In 1943, alone, Disney
produced 3,000,000 feet of film, ninety percent of it for the government.[147]

Wartime Documentary Abroad

Although this chapter is limited to the study of U.S. wartime
documentary, some mention should be made of the war documentary efforts
in England. At the outbreak of World War II, Britain possessed a vigorous tradition of documentary film making extending back ten years. The
Ministry of Information was responsible for government documentary,
with the Films Division under J. L. Beddington doing the actual production.[148] In the early years of the war, the Division of Films
concentrated on short five-minute films. By 1942, when they were discontinued, eighty-six of them had been made. The five-minute shorts
were replaced by monthly fifteen-minute films, of which thirty-seven
were produced. The first two types were distributed free to cinemas.[149]
There were also a number of two three-reel films and of course a steady
stream of non-theatrical films designed for specific audiences.

The Ministry's official film producing unit was the Crown Film
Unit, a re-creation of the GPO unit which was responsible for most of the
early documentary work in Britain and for the most important war documentaries, the feature-length films. This production accounted for about
ten percent of the film work of the MOI. The other ninety percent was
commissioned from various commercial producers.[150] Films such as
Coastal Command, Desert Victory, Fires Were Started, London Can
Take It, Western Approaches, and Target for Tonight represent the

best of British documentary during the war. Target for Tonight, seen widely in the United States, earned the highest commendation and received an "Oscar" in 1941.[151]

The estimated weekly audience for war films in Britain was twenty million.[152] By the end of 1945, 726 wartime documentary and information films were completed.[153]

In comparing the British and United States documentary film efforts, Paul Rotha commented, with some degree of bias, that the British spent more time and emphasis on the social effects of war, while the U.S. concentrated more on actual war and combat.[154] Whatever the concentration was in Britain, it remains a fact that the most popular films--those which were rented and for which admission was charged--were films depicting combat and war. These included Target for Tonight, Desert Victory, Western Approaches, etc.

Other countries such as Canada with its "World in Action" series and Germany with its striking campaign films and newsreels, were producing films in great quantity. However, it was the United States, primarily, and Britain that provided the framework for the most extensive and productive wartime documentary film achievement in the history of film.

United States Commercial

Some mention should be made of the commercial motion picture in the United States and how it reacted to and reflected the war.

Pre-World War II

As World War II drew nearer, Hollywood films began to increasingly depict the joys and glamor of military life. As Arthur Knight points out, "Though the government did not actually commission pictures about military life, the studios soon discovered that the War Department was willing to cooperate extensively in the production."[155]

Most of the films were set in a training background. They were for the most part musicals or love stories. Military preparedness was as far as the American people were willing to go.

However, by 1940, with war in Europe raging, the films of Hollywood began to take on more serious tones. Films such as Hitchcock's Foreign Correspondent were examples of the change in theme.

As Arthur Knight points out, during the period of "lend-lease" and "bundles for Britain," Hollywood films acted as a sort of orientation course for the American public, introducing them to future allies and exposing future enemies.[156] During this time Hollywood produced such films as A Yank in the RAF, This Above All, Mrs. Miniver, and Journey for Margaret. The Nazis soon began to appear as villains in such films as The Mortal Storm and Man Hunt.[157]

But until Pearl Harbor, the United States was technically a neutral nation and the studios walked a straight line, conscious of economic reprisals "propaganda" films could invoke across the world.

World War II

Once the United States was committed to war, all restraints vanished. German and Japanese became the stock villains in film after film such as Hitler's Children, Behind the Rising Sun and others.

Other films such as <u>Mission to Moscow</u>, <u>The Moon is Down</u> and <u>This Land</u> <u>is Mine</u> glorified the fighting allies.[158]

Like the "Why We Fight" films these films did not seek to glorify war. Instead, they stressed the average American's dislike for killing and bloodshed. They stressed the nature of the people of the United States and the allied countries.

SUMMARY

There were essentially two main thrusts of the documentary film during war, especially observable during World War II. The first is military, the second, civilian.

The civilian effort in World War II took place almost exclusively within the structure of the OWI and the CIAA. The two main documentary efforts here were Robert Riskin's OWI Overseas Branch and Julien Bryan's Film Division in the CIAA. Both units produced notable documentaries. The best films that emerged from these two groups were true social statements designed to influence. They were propaganda designed to persuade and convince, not merely pictorial newspapers or beautiful filmic episodes.

However, the most notable use of the documentary approach occurred in the military. Two notable achievements, above all, present themselves. The first is Capra's "Why We Fight" series. This group of films is generally acknowledged, even by such grudging critics as Paul Rotha, to be the best example of documentary to come out of the war. The second achievement is the historical information campaign films of John Ford, John Huston, William Wyler and others. Such films as

Memphis Belle, The Battle of San Pietro and the True Glory represent
some of the finest examples of that form of film so aptly described
by Grierson as "the creative treatment of actuality."

There was, of course, a much greater use of film, of all types,
in World War II than at any other time in history. However, as Richard
Griffith correctly observed, most of these productions did not fall
under the "historic reading of documentary."[159] The main objective
of documentary film before World War II, and indeed the essential
criterion for any documentary film, is that it extend experience,
suggest conclusions, stimulate ideas and change or confirm attitudes.
Except for the "Why We Fight" series, the historical campaign films,
some of the OWI Overseas and the CIAA films, this was not the case
with most wartime factual films.

Themes

In terms of themes or general style, the factual films in war
are difficult to hold to any single emphasis. That they did exercise
more sobriety and place more emphasis on facts and information than
their World War I counterparts is apparent. Beyond this they are
difficult to categorize. However, several themes or patterns are
discernible. Among them are the tendency toward personalization--
to show closeups of faces and people--and the tendency to show the
common bonds that unite a fighting people--people fighting under God
for a just cause.

However, if any one pattern or theme emerged most clearly from
the many films of World War II it was that America basically hated
war, that war was thrust upon it. Time after time, especially in the

"Why We Fight" series and other orientation films, the theme is carried
across that we did not want war and were fighting only because it was
forced upon us. Not strictly a pacifist stance, it resembled the
righteous wrath of a just and forbearing people finally forced to
defend themselves and pick up the sword from struggling allies. The
emphasis placed on the "cause" was especially significant. As Charles
Hoben observed:

> Behind the development in Army films was a broad
> concept of the dynamics of human behavior, an empirical
> understanding of the reasons why people behave as they
> do, and a positive approach to the direction and control
> of human behavior . . . Its films . . . dealt not only
> with what men must know, but also what men must do and
> why they must do it. In order that its men be brought
> to a mental state where they were willing to make the
> sacrifices they were called upon to make and to perform
> the duties they were called upon to perform. The Army
> made and used films which showed the nobility of the
> cause in which they were engaged, the morality of indi-
> vidual conduct under stress of strong emotion, the
> progress of their fellow men in furthering the cause
> in other ways and the principles and performances of
> technical operations that must be learned and performed
> with speed and efficiency to ensure the triumph of the
> cause the men were called upon to defend.[160]

Beyond themes and general patterns, perhaps the greatest single
area of achievement in documentary film in World War II was the sheer
size of the operation, the number of people who participated in the
movement and who viewed the product. As numerous critics have stated,
the Second World War gave non-theatrical films their greatest chance
for service and their greatest public recognition. War is essentially
a time for action and there is basic agreement on immediate goals of
action. These two trends gave documentary film the framework in which
it flourished and grew as never before or since. Wartime government
sponsorship provided the vastly increased opportunity to experiment

while the necessity for speed provided the needed impetus for the documentary film's success.

This, then, is the general scope of documentary in war. To be sure, the effort was at times uncoordinated and overlapping; but it did have significant moments of distinct quality, and above all it had tremendous volume and public recognition.

[1]Richard Griffith in Cecile Starr, _Ideas on Film_ (New York: Funk & Wagnalls Co., 1951).

[2]Orton H. Hicks, "Army Pictures Reach 'Round the World," _Business Screen_, VII (1945), p. 53.

[3]_Ibid._, p. 74.

[4]Frank Liberman, "A History of Army Photography," _Business Screen_, VII (1945), p. 16.

[5]_Ibid._

[6]_Ibid._, p. 17.

[7]George Creel, _How We Advertised America_ (New York: Harper & Brothers, 1920), p. 117.

[8]Terry Ramsaye, _A Million and One Nights_ (New York: Simon & Schuster, 1926), p. 781.

[9]Creel, p. 119.

[10]_Ibid._, p. 120.

[11]_Ibid._, p. 121.

[12]_Ibid._

[13]_Ibid._, p. 122.

[14]_Ibid._

[15]Ramsaye, p. 784.

[16]Creel, p. 123.

[17]_Ibid._, p. 124.

[18]_Ibid._, p. 125.

[19]Ramsaye, p. 784.

[20]Creel, p. 126.

[21]Ibid.

[22]Ibid.

[23]Ibid., p. 117.

[24]Ramsaye, p. 786.

[25]Liberman, p. 17.

[26]Ibid., p. 95.

[27]"On the Production Line," Business Screen, VII (1945), p. 24.

[28]Liberman, p. 94.

[29]Ibid., p. 95.

[30]Ibid., p. 94.

[31]Ibid., p. 95.

[32]James V. Clarke, "Signal Corps Army Pictorial Service in World War II, 1 September 1939-15 August 1945" (Signal Corps Historical Monograph, Signal Corps Historical Section File, National Archives, Washington, D.C., 1945), p. 018.

[33]"Military Films," Film News, I (November, 1940), p. 4.

[34]Liberman, p. 95.

[35]Clarke, p. 019.

[36]Ibid., p. 038.

[37]Ibid., p. 003.

[38]Ibid., p. 020.

[39]"Military Films," Film News, I (November, 1940), p. 4.

[40]"Health For Defense," Film News, II (May, 1941), p. 4.

[41]Paul Rotha and Richard Griffith, The Film Till Now (London: Spring Books, 1967), p. 459.

[42]R. Keith Lane, "The O.F.F.," Public Opinion Quarterly, VI (Summer, 1942), 204.

[43]Cedric Larson, "The Domestic Motion Picture Work of the Office of War Information," Hollywood Quarterly, III (1947-48), p. 434.

[44] Ibid., p. 436.

[45] Ibid., pp. 436-437.

[46] Arthur L. Mayer, "Fact into Film," Public Opinion Quarterly, VIII (Summer, 1944), 211.

[47] Richard MacCann, "Documentary Film and Democratic Government: An Administrative History from Pare Lorentz to John Huston" (unpublished Ph.D. dissertation, Harvard, 1951), p. 278.

[48] Larson, p. 436.

[49] Rotha and Griffith, p. 311.

[50] Larson, p. 435.

[51] "National Defense," Film News, I (October, 1940), p. 1.

[52] "Coordinator Shapes War Film Policy," Film News, III (February, 1942), p. 1.

[53] Larson, p. 439.

[54] Ibid., p. 437.

[55] Mayer, p. 211.

[56] George Thompson and Dixie Harris, The Signal Corps: The Outcome (Washington, D.C.: U.S. Government Printing Office, 1966), p. 544.

[57] "Films for Civilian Defense," Film News, III (Late Summer, 1942), p. 3.

[58] Rotha and Griffith, p. 344.

[59] Ibid., p. 346.

[60] Andrew Buchanan, The Film in Education (London: Phoenix House, Ltd., 1951), p. 61.

[61] Clarke, p. 037.

[62] Ibid., p. 038.

[63] Ibid.

[64] George Thompson, Dixie Harris, Pauline Oakes, and Dulany Terrett, The Signal Corps: The Test (Washington, D.C.: U.S. Government Printing Office, 1957), p. 390.

[65] Dulany Terrett, The Signal Corps: The Emergency (Washington, D.C.: U.S. Government Printing Office, 1956), p. 224.

[66] Ibid.

[67] Ibid., p. 226.

[68] Ibid., pp. 227-28.

[69] Ibid., p. 228.

[70] Ibid.

[71] Ibid.

[72] Thompson, Harris, Oakes and Terrett, p. 390.

[73] Thompson and Harris, p. 547.

[74] Ibid., p. 542.

[75] Ibid.

[76] Ibid.

[77] Ibid., p. 560.

[78] Ibid., pp. 560-61.

[79] Charles Hoban, Movies That Teach (New York: Dryden Press, 1946), pp. 22-23.

[80] Thompson and Harris, p. 548.

[81] Clarke, p. 007.

[82] Thompson, Harris, Oakes and Terrett, p. 426.

[83] Thompson and Harris, p. 548.

[84] Ibid., p. 547.

[85] Ibid., p. 549.

[86] Ibid.

[87] Ibid., pp. 549-50.

[88] Ibid., p. 550.

[89] Ibid., p. 551.

[90] Ibid.

[91] Emanuel Cohen, "Film is a Weapon," Business Screen, VII (1945), p. 43.

[92] Ibid.

[93] Clarke, p. 175.

[94] Thompson, Harris, Oakes and Terrett, p. 416.

[95] Thompson and Harris, p. 556.

[96] Ibid., pp. 557-58.

[97] Thompson, Harris, Oakes and Terrett, p. 416.

[98] Ibid., p. 416.

[99] Rotha and Griffith, p. 463.

[100] Ibid.

[101] Memorandum, Frank Capra to General Osborn, March 4, 1942, National Archives, Washington, D.C., Capra file.

[102] Rotha and Griffith, p. 351.

[103] Thompson and Harris, p. 558.

[104] Ibid.

[105] Rotha and Griffith, p. 353.

[106] Ibid.

[107] Mayer, p. 218.

[108] James Agee, review of the "Army-Navy Screen Magazine," in The Nation (March 4, 1944), p. 288.

[109] Ibid.

[110] Thompson and Harris, pp. 558-59.

[111] Ibid.

[112] Thompson, Harris, Oakes and Terrett, p. 418.

[113]Ibid.

[114]Mayer, p. 219.

[115]Ibid.

[116]Hicks, p. 74.

[117]"Navy Trains with Films," Film News, III (November 26, 1942), p. 4.

[118]Ibid.

[119]John Winnie, private interview held during meeting of National Association of Broadcasters, Chicago, Illinois, April, 1968.

[120]Orville Goldner, "The Story of Navy Training Films," Business Screen, VI (1945), p. 29.

[121]Ibid.

[122]Col. M. Nelson, "Marines Make Motion Pictures," Film News, III (March, 1942), p. 2.

[123]Thompson, Harris, Oakes and Terrett, p. 392.

[124]Ibid., p. 394.

[125]Thompson and Harris, p. 552.

[126]Ibid., p. 555.

[127]Creel, p. 274.

[128]Ibid.

[129]Joseph Barnes, "Fighting with Information: OWI Overseas," Public Opinion Quarterly, VII (Spring, 1943), 34.

[130]"Film Story of OWI Overseas," Film News, V (November, 1944), p. 3.

[131]Robert Katz and Nancy Katz, "Documentary in Transition, Part I: The United States," Hollywood Quarterly, III (1947-48), 428.

[132]"Film Story of OWI Overseas," Film News, V (November, 1944), p. 3.

[133]Ibid.

[134]Ibid.

[135] Ibid.

[136] Ibid.

[137] Ibid.

[138] Robert C. Maroney, "Films in the Other Americas," Film News, VI (April, 1945), p. 2.

[139] "Bryan's Films Lead CIAA Program," Film News, III (November 3, 1943), p. 2.

[140] Ibid.

[141] Ibid.

[142] Mayer, p. 220.

[143] "Bryan's Films Lead CIAA Program," Film News, III (November 3, 1943), p. 2.

[144] New York Times, February 7, 1943, II, p. 3.

[145] Mayer, p. 220.

[146] Ibid.

[147] New York Times, February 7, 1943, II, p. 3.

[148] H. D. Waley, "British Documentaries and the War Effort," Public Opinion Quarterly, VI (Winter, 1942), 605.

[149] "Pep Broadsheet on British Documentary Films," Film News, VI (May, 1945), p. 9.

[150] Waley, p. 606.

[151] Ibid.

[152] "Pep Broadsheet on British Documentary Films," Film News, VI (May, 1945), p. 9.

[153] Ibid.

[154] Rotha and Griffith, p. 248.

[155] Arthur Knight, The Liveliest Art (New York: The Macmillan Co., 1957), p. 243.

[156] Ibid.

85

157Ibid.

158Ibid., p. 244.

159Rotha and Griffith, p. 358.

160Hoban, p. 22.

CHAPTER III

A HISTORY OF THE "WHY WE FIGHT" SERIES

This chapter is divided into two parts. The first portion is a review of the events leading up to the "Why We Fight" series, particularly the increased emphasis on the need for morale in the armed forces. The second part is a history of the "Why We Fight" series itself. Emphasis is on the origin and objectives of the series, the production, distribution and utilization of the films, and reaction to and critical evaluation of the films.

INCREASED EMPHASIS ON THE NEED FOR MORALE

On August 18, 1941, the United States House of Representatives met to vote on a crucial issue: the extension of the Selective Service Act of September 16, 1940, whereby the new American "draft army" might be kept in force. Draftees would now be required to serve for two years rather than the one year specified in the original measure. The vote was 203 yes, 202 no.[1] By this legislative eyelash, some measure of this country's reluctance for international commitment was dramatically demonstrated.

The crushing blow of Pearl Harbor three and one-half months later was to stagger a nation steeped in unsophisticated cynicism regarding world politics and the affairs of nations. The generation that was to fight World War II had been

86

. . . brought up in the intellectual and moral
confusions of the twenties and the depression of
the thirties. So-called intellectuals had dinned
their ears that we were suckers in World War I, and
that other nations were leeches sucking our blood.
In the future, we ought to be "realistic."[2]

The American citizen was determined that he would not be "sucked

n" by propaganda, a word made nefarious by Herr Goebbels.

In the course of the re-evaluation which followed
the first World War, many Americans were exposed to
a de-bunking process which challenged the worthwhile-
ness of the most recent major cause to which they had
given their allegiance. The moral drawn from this
was that people became converted to supporting causes
by a kind of trickery--"propaganda"--and that it was
therefore wise to be on one's guard against being
taken in by propaganda. As a result, the very discussion of abstract ideas, especially where they
concerned themselves with values, was suspect. If
a label had to be put to it, it might be said that
the dominant philosophical tone of the period was a
variety of positivistic materialism which belittled
if it did not deny the validity of any concern with
values.[3]

Despite this concern with propaganda, there was no lack of informa-

ion in the mass media as to what the war was about. The public was in-

ormed of totalitarian terror, Fascist brutality, the threat to democracy

nd the "American way of life."

The radio, newspaper and motion picture provided a steady flow

f information prior to our entry into the war on the plight of the

rench and British, the devastation of China and Mussolini's war on

thiopia. Radio especially came into its own as a news medium, quickly

nd comprehensively reporting the progress of the war.

These war communiques were increasingly supplemented by personal

ye witness reports of American correspondents. Names such as Edward R.

urrow and William Shirer became commonplace to the American radio audience. These reports became less objective as the course of the war progressed. With the appearance of occasional dramatizations such as "The March of Time's" Inside Nazi Germany, it became clear that some effort was being made to "take sides."

After December 7, 1941, the news media were quickly mobilized to provide the most comprehensive and up-to-date coverage of the current state of the war as well as attempting to instill within the American people certain beliefs about the war and why they were fighting. The formation of the Office of War Information on June 13, 1942, was a key factor in this dual mission.

Radio played a significant role in this mission. Unlike the other mass media--the press and motion picture--this was radio's first war. It was employed extensively as a medium of information and propaganda. A prime example of this was the group of plays "The Free World Presents," broadcast over NBC Blue as a joint presentation of the Office of War Information, the Hollywood Writers Mobilization and the Hollywood Victory Committee. Their purpose was to ". . . prevent evil from gaining sole mastery of the earth and to wage an end to the war forced upon us, for the sake of mankind's honor and for the preservation of our own lives."[4]

The motion picture and press no less adamantly pursued the course of informing and persuading the American people. "The March of Time's" screen journalism hit hard at the very roots of fascist tyranny and the editorial pages of the nation's most influential newspapers, although basically more conservative, refused to sit on the sidelines.

However, in December, 1943, Cecil Brown reported in <u>Colliers</u>:

> Confusion over what we are fighting to eradicate
> from the world and what we propose to substitute
> in its place prevails throughout the country . . .
> I asked hundreds of people from coast to coast:
> "What is Fascism?" . . . people could not agree,
> or had no idea whatever.[5]

Key personnel with the ability to evaluate the situation realized
at the war would be long and costly. The initial fury from the shock
the attack would wear thin, and something more in the form of a
commitment to lasting values would be needed if national morale was to
sustained.

Thus, the men of the United States Army were recruited from a
tion possessing little articulated ideology. The average man on the
reet, being a product of an isolationist atmosphere, could not be ex-
cted to acquire automatically an international frame of mind upon
tering the Army, especially as an unwilling draftee. Private groups
ch as The Committee for National Morale were studying the causes of
tional confusion and were greatly concerned over the attitudes of
oops. It was becoming clearer to the public and to the Army that
e attitudes of troops were closely related to those of the public
d that morale was a complicated matter indeed.[6]

E. A. Steckel and K. E. Appel, writing in the September, 1942,
sue of the <u>American Journal of Psychiatry</u>, pointed out:

> One of the most important phenomena in the present
> world conflict is the use of psychology in affecting
> thought, feelings, and behavior on a mass scale.
> There is a new emphasis on will to fight rather than
> simply on ability to fight. What are the elements
> of this will to fight, or morale?

> Each soldier should know what he is fighting for.
> Each civilian should know what he is fighting for.
> We need a slogan.
> We must develop anger at the enemy.
> We must instill the specific fear of the conse-
> quences of defeat.
> We must develop in each citizen the willingness
> to sacrifice himself for the good of the whole.
> Develop confidence in self.
> Develop confidence in our leaders.
>
> . . . We must use propaganda emotionally . . . .[17]

The leaders of the armed forces fully realized the problem and early sought means to instill in the draftee dedication to a cause which would transcend the simple necessity of fighting just to get the war over with.

History of Morale Activity in the Armed Forces

Until the last months of World War I, the provision of any service to soldiers other than those directly related to training or combat were not considered part of the Army's responsibilities.

Civil War

In every major war in the nation's history, civilian groups had been formed to help the troops, beginning in the days of the Committee of Pennsylvania Women who raised $300,000 in 1780 to purchase clothing for soldiers.[8] In the Civil War the Sanitary Commission which provided welfare supplies as well as medical attention was essential to the physical well-being of the troops. Civilian organizations in the North prepared and distributed pamphlets and newspapers sympathetic to the Union cause, in opposition to Copperhead defeatism. The Reading Agent for the Army of the Cumberland alone distributed 35,000 magazines by late 1863, and set up in camps a loan library system of 250 libraries

Several other civilian groups were active in attempting to combat the spread of Copperhead literature; but even in the bleak days of 1862-63, President Lincoln alone could place restrictions on such activity, because such activity was deemed political and not the responsibility of the Army.[10]

World War I

It was not, then, until World War I that the Army came to recognize the need for assuming a direct responsibility for the many activities which were loosely defined as morale. Just before the end of the war, a Morale Branch of the Army was established in the General Staff to coordinate the work of civilian welfare agencies and to consider and take appropriate action on other factors which influence the morale of the Army, including the undertaking of experimental studies. This work might have had important implications for the Army during peacetime, but the drastic curtailment of appropriations to the Army naturally struck hard at any unit so lately established as was the Morale Branch.[11]

World War II

Little was accomplished or even considered concerning an Army morale program until early 1941. A Morale Division of the Adjutant General's Office was established in July, 1940, with Morale Publicity one of its five functions. Although it appeared as though the War Department planned to inaugurate an information program for the troops, this section was primarily a public relations office for the War Department. It had neither official responsibility for, nor intention of, expanding into an education or orientation program.[12]

However, the War Department was aware that morale was not simply a matter of good chow and letters from home. Two conferences held in February and March of 1941 point this out.

The first was a conference of morale officers held in Washington, D.C., February 25-28, 1941. The conference pointed to the somewhat obvious fact that the War Department's existing machinery was not adequate to "enable the Chief of the Morale Division at all times to know the state of morale of the Army."[13]

A second conference of Army Public Relations Officers was held in Washington, D.C., March 11-14, 1941. Practically every phase of publicity concerning the Army was thrashed out. Chief of Staff General George C. Marshall pointed out during the conference that the primary purpose of public relations is to stimulate and maintain high morale in the armed forces and in civilian life. Marshall stated:

> . . . morale is of the highest importance. As a
> matter of fact, it is no exaggeration to say that the
> materiel, the munitions we turn out, will be of little
> avail without high morale in the personnel to handle
> them. The excellence of training of that personnel
> depends greatly upon morale . . .[14]

Speaking before the same conference, Secretary of War Stimson also keynoted the subject of morale.

> The success of an army depends upon its morale . . .
> Nothing can undermine this morale . . . so rapidly and
> so thoroughly as the feeling that they are being de-
> ceived; that they are not being given the real facts
> about their progress and the progress of the cause
> which they are preparing to defend. This is true even
> in the case of the army of a free people . . . There-
> fore, the army of such a country does not need to be
> bolstered up by false propaganda. What they want is
> to be sure of the fair truth; and, if they feel they
> are getting that, they will carry through to the end.

> Therefore, it is vital that both the army and the
> people behind it must know the real basic facts,
> free from any false exaggerations either one way
> or the other.[15]

As a result of these conferences and further study of the problem, a Morale Branch of the Army was established on March 14, 1941, functioning directly under the supervision of the Chief of Staff.[16]

The summer of 1941 brought further unrest and concern over this nation's stand in both civilian and army quarters. This was witnessed by the intense debate surrounding and narrow victory for the extension of the Selective Service Act and threats of OHIO ("Over the Hill in October") by draftees who thought one year was enough. As Time stated in August, 1941:

> The low state of Army morale was merely brought into
> the open by the draft-extension bill. Its roots went
> back much further . . . The great bulk of civilian
> soldiers had little pride of outfit, little joy of
> service. Like many soldiers . . . they wanted to go
> home.[17]

Time observed that this condition was witnessed by uniformed men at a Mississippi camp booing newsreel shots of President Roosevelt and General Marshall and cheering a speech by isolationist Senator Hiram Johnson.[18]

Thus, the importance of troop understanding of the reasons for their year of service as well as the need for civilian support of the War Department's efforts was virtually forced on the Army by the public discussion and debate of the need for the Selective Service, as well as the general unrest among members of the Army.

A significant step in combating the problem of morale was the appointment of noted sociologist Frederick Osborn to head the Morale

Division. As was pointed out by George McMillan in Public Opinion
Quarterly:

> The very best the War Department can do will be
> needed to meet the morale problem it faces during
> the second year of service for its' draftees, if
> newspaper and magazine reports are accurate. The
> appointment of Frederick Osborn . . . to head the
> morale division is evidence that this is recognized
> by the general staff.[19]

A further step in the battle for the civilian and military mind
was the establishment of the Research and Analysis Branch of the
Bureau of Public Relations of the War Department.[20]

Thus, four basic factors underlay the expansion of the services
of the Morale Branch to include mental stimulation and training in
addition to recreation and amusement. They were:

1) The intellectual qualities and interests of the new
personnel brought into the Branch;

2) The stimulus of public interest and criticism;

3) The objective information on basic factors affecting
soldier morale developed by research studies on soldier
attitudes; and

4) The growing unrest and the needs of an expanding army,
as developed in the field and reported back to Washington.[21]

A critical step in the expansion of morale activities in the Army
occurred just three weeks before Pearl Harbor. General Marshall called
a conference on November 18, 1941, to initiate an Army-wide program of
orientation on the reasons for military service. The responsibility
for the program was first assigned to the Bureau of Public Relations,
but was later transferred to the Morale Branch. The program officially
opened December 15, 1941.[22]

The emphasis on information and orientation increased throughout the war, culminating in the formation in 1943, of an Information and Education Division of the Army. This represented the final step in a long road toward realization of the importance of soldier attitude and knowledge concerning the war and its causes.

At the end of the war, the Army Orientation Course played a major role in explaining the principles and procedures of the Army's discharge plan, as it had played a similar part during the war in stimulating understanding of the causes and the progress of the war. As the study of Information and Education activities during World War II stated,

> . . . by the end of the war there were thousands of men whose range of thinking about personal, national and international problems had been widened and stimulated. . . . It was widely recognized in and out of the Army that the citizen soldier needed to know why he was in uniform and why he was assigned to his particular duties, if he was to reach maximum effectiveness.[23]

THE "WHY WE FIGHT" SERIES

Background

One of the early means of implementing the morale program was a series of orientation lectures delivered by a corps of speakers to troops throughout the country. The program was inaugurated in 1940 under the supervision of the Bureau of Public Relations of the War Department General Staff.[24]

However, dissatisfaction with the method of presentation soon became apparent. To historians, scholars and students of world politics, the background of events leading up to war presented in lecture form was perhaps fascinating, but "to soldiers bone-tired from their initial encounter with basic training the information proved baffling, bewildering or just boring."[25]

Marshall, himself, was keenly aware of these deficiencies. He stated:

> I personally found the lectures of officers to the men, as to what they were fighting for and what the enemy had done, so unsatisfactory because of the mediocrity of presentation that I directed the preparation of this series of films . . . The responsibility for the films was purely mine.[26]

Marshall was aware of the limitations of the lecture and was eager to expand the already existing training film program to include orientation films. Thus, the "Why We Fight" series was created.

Beginning

Some confusion exists as to the actual start of the program, especially concerning the arrival--both the date and the means--of Frank Capra, who was not only to direct the "Why We Fight" films, but eventually to head up the Army's entire film program. Much of this can perhaps be traced to immediate post-Pearl Harbor confusion caused by, among other things, literally thousands of programs previously existing only on paper, being implemented in a few days.

The most reasonably accurate account as pieced together from various memoranda and directives points to December 10, 1941, as the beginning. On December 9, Brigadier General F. H. Osborn, Chief of the Morale Branch (later Special Services), met with Colonel Schlosberg of the Army Pictorial Service to get the program moving. Schlosberg agreed to try to find a qualified person from the motion picture

ndustry to direct a series of orientation films. On December 10,
941, a memorandum from Osborn with the concurrence of the Director
f the Bureau of Public Relations requested that the Chief Signal
fficer secure an immediate appropriation of $150,000 for the prepara-
ion of orientation films. This appropriation was granted some three
onths later.[27]

Meanwhile, the critical need was for a qualified individual to
irect the program. As was mentioned previously, various accounts
xist as to exactly when and how Frank Capra assumed the directorship.
ne account states that the Signal Corps requested him to apply for a
ommission on December 8, 1941.[28] Another version states that on
ecember 12, 1941, Capra offered his services to the War Department
nd, reputedly at the direct order of President Roosevelt, was commis-
ioned a Major and put in charge of the War Department's film program.[29]
lso, the aforementioned meeting of Osborn and Schlosberg on December 9,
941, was to have resulted in a search for a qualified individual to
ead the program.[30] Yet still another account gathered from a personal
nterview with Colonel R. C. Barrett (Retired) sets forth the account
hat Capra was a personal friend of Marshall, who asked him to direct
he films.[31]

The most reasonably accurate account, as set down in an official
emorandum from General F. H. Osborn, Chief of Special Services, seems
 be that Osborn asked the Signal Corps to induct Frank Capra into
he Army and assign him to Special Services. Capra reported for duty
bruary 14, 1942, and was immediately made Chief of the Film Produc-
on Section of Special Services.[32]

Some two weeks after Capra reported for duty, General Marshall sent for Capra and General Osborn, and for an hour discussed with them the importance of "maintaining morale and instilling loyalty and discipline into the civilian army being assembled to make war on professional enemies."[33] He gave Capra and Osborn a general order to do all they could with motion pictures to accomplish these purposes and emphasized the necessity for speed.[34]

Taking the cue from Marshall, seven basic films were produced for the Special Services by the Signal Corps: Prelude to War, The Nazis Strike, Divide and Conquer, The Battle of Britain, The Battle of Russia, The Battle of China and War Comes to America. They were called the "Why We Fight" series.

Purpose and Objectives

Although the themes and purposes of the individual films will be discussed extensively in a later chapter, some mention as to the general purposes and objectives of the series is essential to an understanding of its place in the Army's morale program.

Again, several interpretations exist as to the exact nature of the series' purpose and objectives. Accounts basically agree that the films were designed to motivate the men and to provide them with information as to why they were fighting.

Hovland, Lumsdaine and Sheffield, in their book Experiments on Mass Communication, state that two basic assumptions appeared to underli the preparation of the films. The first was that a sizeable segment of the draftee population lacked knowledge concerning the national and international events that resulted in America's entrance into the war.

The second was that a knowledge of these events would in some measure

lead men to accept more willingly the transformation from civilian to

Army life and their duties as soldiers.[35] They further state on the

basis of their experimentation with the "Why We Fight" films that the

purposes of the films were essentially that of the orientation program

as a whole.[36] These purposes, as set forth in a directive from the

General Staff, were:

1. To foster a firm belief in the right for which we fight

2. To foster a realization that we are up against a tough job

3. To initiate a determined confidence in our own ability and
   the ability of our comrades and leaders to do the job that
   has to be done

4. To instill a feeling of confidence, insofar as is possible
   under the circumstances, in the integrity and fighting
   ability of our allies

5. To create a resentment, based on knowledge of the facts,
   against our enemies who have made it necessary for us to
   fight

6. To foster a belief that through military victory, the
   political achievement of a better world order is possible.[37]

The essential purpose of the films is also indicated by General

Marshall's statement in the opening title of the first film, Prelude

to War:

> This film, the first of a series, has been prepared
> by the War Department to acquaint members of the Army
> with factual information as to the causes, the events
> leading up to our entry into the war, and to the
> principles for which we are fighting. A knowledge
> of these facts is an indispensable part of military
> training and merits the thoughtful consideration of
> every American Soldier.[38]

Capra, himself, stated, "We lost the peace the last time because

the men of the armed forces were uninformed about what they went to war for--and the nature and type of the enemy they were fighting. None of us here thinks that is going to happen again."[39]

However, perhaps the most accurate and complete statement of purpose is found in a memorandum from Capra to Lowell Mellet, dated May 1, 1942. The two main objectives of the films, according to Capra, were to: (1) win the war, (2) win the peace.[40]

Capra further stated that in order to carry out the above objectives "We must set our sights on certain specific ends and means."[41] First of all the films should create a will to win by:

1. Making clear the enemies' ruthless objectives;

2. Promoting confidence in the ability of our armed forces to win;

3. Showing clearly that we are fighting for the existence of our country and all our freedoms;

4. Showing clearly how we would lose our freedoms if we lost the war; and

5. Making clear we carry the torch of freedom.[42]

Capra also stated that the films should create a desire to insure against the recurrence of world war by:

1. Explaining and exposing aggression and conquest;

2. Showing the necessity for better understanding between nations and peoples;

3. Showing the necessity for outlawing conquest and exploitation by the few;

4. Showing the necessity for eliminating economic evils;

5. Proclaiming the Four Freedoms; and

6. Promoting democratic principles.[43]

Thus, in summary, orientation films explained the political and social events that caused the war, gave meaning to the tedium of military training and significance to the individual soldier's participation in the war.

Organization of the Film Unit

The organization of the unit assembled to produce the orientation films began with the selection of Frank Capra. He immediately set about collecting personnel and setting up the structure of the unit.

The unit originally began in the Department of Public Relations of the War Department. It remained there during the initial stages of planning and assembling men and material. Some degree of confusion existed at this point. As Arthur Calder-Marshall stated, "Nobody in fact knew what anyone was doing there at the moment. Capra, a master of story-pictures, knew nothing of documentary and was shopping for experience."[44] The initial work was conducted in Washington, D.C. When the first film was ready to be produced, the Army Pictorial Service in early May, 1942, was directed to establish a Signal Corps detachment under the jurisdiction and control of the Chief, Special Services Division, Service of Supply, for the purpose of producing motion pictures with Capra in charge.[45] Capra had no professional production unit in Washington and had to borrow one from the Signal Corps, the personnel of which resented the new Capra unit.[46]

Thus, on June 6, 1942, at the direction of the Commander General, Services of Supply, the 834th Signal Service Photographic Detachment with specially selected personnel was activated for the purpose of producing the orientation films of the "Why We Fight" series. The unit was located in the old Fox studio on Western Avenue in Hollywood.[47]

This detachment, commanded by Capra, operated at first under the jurisdiction and direct control of the Chief of Special Services. The Signal Corps' responsibility was limited to supplying the technicians and assisting upon request. Capra and several other key personnel, however, were commissioned in the Signal Corps from the first.

On September 1, 1943, the memorandum assigning the 834th Signal Service Photographic Detachment to Special Services was rescinded and the unit was assigned to the Army Pictorial Service of the Signal Corps. The Signal Corps, thereafter, produced films for the Special Services Division upon SSD's request, in the same manner as for other agencies in the Army.[48]

In October, 1943, the unit was transferred from Hollywood to the Signal Corps Photographic Center in New York, where it remained for the duration of the war.[49]

Personnel

To carry out the "Why We Fight" objectives, Capra assembled many of the leading motion picture personnel in Hollywood. Other Army personnel were assigned as the project grew. Initially, the 834th unit comprised eight officers and thirty-five enlisted men. The enlisted men were generally old-time Hollywood technicians who were specifically asked to enlist for the job. Most of them were well over 35, including some veterans of World War I. This number was supplemented by several civilians hand-picked by Capra--as were most of the top personnel, both military and civilian. At the peak, Capra had a crew of twenty-five enlisted men cutters with an average of eleven years experience in the cutting rooms of the major studios.[50]

None of these men received any public credit for the films. It was known that Capra was the producer of the series, but individual credits were strictly forbidden by the Army.

The personnel chosen by Capra included seven writers: Leonard Spigelgass, Ted Paramore, John Sandford, Gerald Chodorof, Epstein Bres, Sam K. Lauren and Anthony Veiller. Others engaged in writing and research were William L. Shirer, John Whittacker, Eric Knight and James Hilton. Capra and Anatole Litvak were the directors. Film editors included Academy Award winner William Hornbeck, Henry Burman, Leon Levy and John Hoffman. Dimitri Tiomkin scored and conducted the music. Walter Huston and Anthony Veiller narrated the films. Richard Griffith, noted film historian and critic, was in charge of research. Sam Briskin, former general manager of Columbia Studios, was production manager.[51] Noted documentarists Joris Ivens and Robert Flaherty joined Capra's film unit, but after unsuccessful attempts to produce films left for film posts in the Dutch East Indies and Great Britain, respectively.[52]

Capra, of course, was the key figure in this assemblage. Long one of Hollywood's most successful directors, he won his spurs directing rough and ready melodramas for Columbia and was the director for most of Harry Langdon's films. His series of films, beginning with the successful (nine Academy Awards) It Happened One Night and including

Mr. Deeds Goes to Town, Mr. Smith Goes to Washington and You Can't

Take it With You, set a new style in films aptly entitled "screwball

comedy." As Richard Griffith stated,

> There can be little question that Capra is a first-
> rate film maker. As ingenious as Lubitsch in inventing
> action and business, his most salient talent is that of
> editing. He approaches his films as might Griffith or
> Eisenstein; their issue to him is a matter of analytical
> construction. This editing skill was, above all, the
> basis for the excellence of the 'Why We Fight' films.[53]

Capra personally directed the first three films of the series and

supervised the remaining four. It was he who gave them their distinc-

tive shape based on the editing principle as the defining factor in

the conception and execution of every film. As Griffith stated,

> Many times when a film had been virtually completed
> by others of his staff, he would take it away to the
> cutting rooms for a few days. Screened again, it
> would seem on the surface much the same, yet
> invariably it had acquired a magical coherence and
> cogency which testified eloquently to Capra's editing
> capacity.[54]

In the spring of 1943, Capra received orders to drop his work on

the "Why We Fight" series and rush into production a film on the Tuni-

sian campaign. When Capra returned to the United States, he was put

in charge of all Army Pictorial Service operations and had less and

less to do with any individual films. He now supervised not only the

orientation series, but also training films, combat reports and the

"Army-Navy Screen Magazine." When Capra left the Army in June, 1945,

he was awarded the Distinguished Service Medal and the Legion of Merit.[55]

Production

Planning of the films began immediately after Capra entered the

Army in February, 1942. By the end of April, Hollywood writers under

Capra's guidance had completed a series of scripts based primarily on the Bureau of Public Relation's lectures. <u>Prelude to War</u>, the initial film in the series, was first shown on October 30, 1942.[56] Work proceeded at a rapid pace throughout the war, with the last film, <u>War Comes to America</u>, completed in early 1945.

The script of each film was written primarily by Eric Knight, once one of Hollywood's highest paid and most intelligent writers. At first, detailed scripts and shot listings were prepared, but the task of finding shots in film archives to illustrate these scripts proved extremely difficult. Thereafter, just basic story outlines were constructed, making the job of locating specific shots less difficult.[57]

After the scripts were prepared, the music was created and scored. Dimitri Tiomkin was in complete charge of all music. Shots were then selected to harmonize with the music as well as the story outline.

While the scripts were written in Hollywood, most of the film from which shots were to be selected was located in New York and Washington, D.C. The distance created difficulties as the script writers wrote without detailed information on what film was available. Hence, arguments arose between the writers, who wrote with the assumption that shots were available or could be created to illustrate their scripts, and the researchers, whose task it was to find shots to illustrate the scripts. In 1943, the problem was alleviated to a great extent when the entire 834th Detachment was transferred to New York.[58]

Approximately eighty percent of the film used was obtained from newsreels and library sources. The rest consisted essentially of animated maps, drawings and staged production shots. The following sources and figures indicate some of the wide variety of sources used:

Fox-Movietone News Library - 30,000 feet

Pathe News - 30,000 feet

Art-Kino and the Soviet Embassy - 8,000 feet

British Ministry of Information - 6,000 feet

Australian News Bureau - 4,000 feet

Private film libraries - 10,000 feet[59]

The figures on the amount of film and the sources represent what had been procured as of mid-1942. However, the percentage of film received from these sources remained essentially the same throughout the production of the series. Also to be included in these sources was captured enemy film, which, of course, became available after these initial figures were complied. Some studio production footage was used in all the films as well. Animated maps and drawings were made by Walt Disney under commercial contract.[60]

The cost of the newsreel and private source materials was approximately ten cents a foot for a master copy, while the cost of film from foreign countries involved the cost of the laboratory work alone.[61] Thus, although no actual cost figures except the initial $150,000 appropriation are available, the entire cost of the project was low compared to commercial standards.

The films involved a complicated editing job. After the scripts were completed and basic footage obtained, the material went to Capra

and his crew of cutters headed by William Hornbeck. The basic material
was edited and spliced until it was precision perfect. This took the
most time. Often, as Richard Griffith notes, Capra would take a completed film into the cutting rooms and emerge several days later with
the finished product.[62] The nature of this editing and its contribution to the films' structure and quality will be discussed at length
in Chapter VI.

Distribution

With the Army using not only the "Why We Fight" films, but
countless others, at an unprecedented rate, it became necessary to set
up a separate distribution network under the Signal Corps. This included a central control and supply agency, decentralized depositories
in the various service commands and smaller libraries at posts and
stations.

> Orientation pictures were made available through
> the use of circuits. The facilities of the Army
> Motion Picture Service, Special Services Division,
> were used to make 35mm prints available in post
> theaters within the Zone of the Interior. The 16mm
> prints were also made available to those charged with
> their exhibition through the use of circuits. The
> planning and operation of the 35mm and 16mm circuits
> was an activity of the Signal Corps Photographic
> Center. In overseas theaters 16mm prints were also
> circulated, in some cases by theater Special Services
> organizations and in others by the Signal Corps film
> distribution facilities.[63]

Prelude to War was first shown to the troops October 30, 1942.[64] The
first five films were shown to all Army personnel for the first time
in 1943.[65] The last film, War Comes to America, did not appear until
1945, a year after The Battle of China. The last two films were not

as widely seen as the first five. The Battle of China, beset by
political problems, was, in fact, quickly withdrawn from distribution.

Use

Military

The films were required seeing for all Army personnel before
they went overseas. Unlike entertainment films, they were shown on
duty time since attendance was compulsory by War Department directive.[66]
The total attendance at the seven films was 45,582,127 by July, 1945.[67]
The films were generally shown to the troops as part of an orientation
period which included discussions and lectures as well as the films.
These orientation periods were conducted by Information and Education
Division officers especially trained for their duties.

The films were also viewed by men in the Navy and the Air Force,
although they were not required to view them. Nelson Rockefeller
utilized several of them for the CIAA program in South America. The
films also received wide foreign distribution. All of the films except The Battle of China were translated into Spanish, Portuguese and
French.[68] They were shown widely to Canadian troops, and the British
Ministry of Information and the Australian News Service made extensive
use of them.[69] There were also foreign civilian showings. The Battle
of Britain was shown in British theaters and was highly praised by
Churchill.[70] The Battle of Russia was translated by Russia into a score
of dialects, and carrying a prologue by Marshal Stalin, was shown
throughout the USSR.[71]

Civilian

The greatest single use of the "Why We Fight" films outside the
U.S. Armed Forces was the showing of the series to war workers and the
general public.

The "Why We Fight" series, along with other Army and Navy films,
was released in April, 1943, for exclusive showings in war plants to
raise industrial morale. Contracts for distribution were made with
three national distributors who divided up the country and subcon-
tracted to agencies in various centers. The Army and Navy supplied
prints and made the industrial contacts.[72]

Increasing technical problems involving distribution to industries
and plant manager reluctance to set aside a forty-minute period for
viewing led to the theatrical release of many Army films, including
three of the "Why We Fight" series, Prelude to War, The Battle of
Britain and The Battle of Russia.[73] Originally, the three contractors
distributing films to war plants inherited the national distribution
rights for theatrical showings. However, attention was focused upon
the noncompetitive nature of the rights and soon the films were released through the Office of War Information and the Hollywood War
Activities Committee.[74]

However, the release of the films was clouded by an intense inner
struggle between the Army and the motion picture industry represented
by the War Activities Committee. Lowell Mellet, Coordinator of Government Films, submitted Prelude to War to the WAC who refused it. At
first, Mellet, himself, was reluctant about submitting the film. To
him the sound track was an affront to the American people, and he felt

the story had already been told in Sam Spewack's movie, World at War.[75]
A conference was held in Washington, D.C., with delegates from the Army
and the film industry present. According to Mellet, the Army threatened
to tell the world the industry was trying to suppress Prelude to War,
whereupon Mellet threatened to tell that the Army was trying to impose
a propaganda film on a free industry. The WAC finally agreed to distribute it with predictions that it would be a box-office failure.[76]
Prelude to War was released through 20th-Century-Fox, May 27, 1943.[77]
It was a box-office failure, although highly acclaimed by a majority
of the critics.

Criticism-Reaction
Theatrical Criticism

Professional critical reaction to the films, especially Prelude
to War and The Battle of Russia, was positive. Prelude to War won an
Academy Award in 1943 as the best documentary film.[78] The New York
critics also voted a special award to the U.S. Army Signal Corps for
the "Why We Fight" series.[79] Perhaps the most lucid and insightful
criticism of the "Why We Fight" series came from the noted film critic,
James Agee. He had occasion to comment upon several of the films,
including Prelude to War, The Battle of Britain and The Battle of Russia.
He described The Battle of Britain as "one hour's calculated hammering
of the eye and ear that can tell you more about the battle than you are
ever likely otherwise to suspect, short of having been there."[80] He
described The Battle of Russia as a lucid piece of exposition cut
purely and resourcefully--and next to The Birth of a Nation, the best

and most important war film ever made in this country.[81] Paul Rotha

stated that the introduction of USSR feature directors into documentary

production was strongly influenced by Capra's success with The Battle

of Russia, which was extremely popular in Russia.[82]

Of course, Agee, as well as other critics, took the films to task

occasionally, especially for their extreme verbosity. Other frequent

comments included "overgeneralization," and "lack of intelligence."

Agee thought that Prelude to War's repeated references to a "Mr. John Q.

Public" were embarrassing, ". . . for they betrayed an underestimation

of the audience. . . ."[83] Again, as with the general troop reaction,

criticism was also leveled against several of the "production shots"

for being "stagey" and lacking forcefulness.

The films' essential purpose, however, was not to be acclaimed

as critical masterpieces and to win awards. Their purpose was to

inform and to convince--to increase factual knowledge about the events

leading up to the war and to motivate the soldier to greater participa-

tion in the war and better acceptance of his role as a soldier. The

extent to which the films succeeded in this dual purpose is somewhat

inconclusive. However, it is well researched.

Troop Reaction and Evaluation

Troop reaction to the films was mixed. Most of the men expressed

an expected preference for the films over the lectures. Several of the

films were auditioned at various Army posts across the country before

being sent into general troop distribution. According to one account,

at one of the posts the men marched into the post theater prepared for

another orientation lecture on some phase of the war. Some of them, from long practice, fell asleep in their seats before the theater filled. Instead of a lecture, the men saw Prelude to War. When it was over, they were awake and applauding.[84]

The Experimental Section of the Research Branch in the War Department's Information and Education Division conducted a series of studies involving the first four films of the "Why We Fight" series. The Experimental Section was, in fact, perhaps partially responsible for the series in the first place. They first undertook a preliminary study to obtain information on the desirability of using documentary films for orientation instead of lectures by officers. Following this study, which pointed to a desire and need for films, the "Why We Fight" series was initiated.[85] As a sequel to the earlier study the Experimental Section was called upon to evaluate the first four films of the series. The basic reason for the research was to evaluate the effectiveness of the films in imparting information about the background of the war and in effecting changes in attitudes toward the war.[86]

The basic procedure followed by the Experimental Section in testing the films involved an experimental group that saw a film, a control group that did not see the film, and a check-list questionnaire that was administered to both groups which sought to measure the men's knowledge and opinions on subjects related to the film.[87]

This study revealed that the most frequent favorable comment was the entertaining and interesting nature of the films. There was little doubt that the films were better than the lectures in their ability to gain and maintain attention. However, other aspects of the films were not so well appreciated. The most consistent criticism from film to

film was the amount of "faked" or "untrue" material arising out of
the repeated use of identical shots from several different films.
The criticism of "onesidedness" was also fairly frequent, especially
concerning The Battle of Britain.[88]

There were faults in the films, to be sure, as there were in the
entire orientation program. However, even with imperfections, a majority of the men who encountered the films liked them. Eighty percent
of the men viewing Prelude to War said they liked it, "yes, very much."
Most men in units which used the orientation program felt they were
better informed because of it.[89]

The results were somewhat inconclusive. The "Why We Fight"
films had marked effects on the men's knowledge of factual material
concerning events leading up to the war. In fact, "correct" information was learned well enough to be remembered a week later by a majority
of the men tested.[90] Thus, as a teaching tool, the films were highly
effective.

However, as a tool for changing opinions and attitudes they were
less effective, and in one key area, had no effect whatsoever.

> The films had some marked effects on opinions where
> the . . . opinion item was prepared on the basis of
> film-content analysis and anticipated opinion change
> from such analysis. Such opinion changes were,
> however, less frequent and in general less marked
> than changes in factual knowledge.[91]

The films also had little effect on opinions of a more general nature
concerning the war. They had no effect on the men's general motivation
to serve as soldiers, which was considered the ultimate objective of
the orientation program.[92]

Several hypotheses were offered concerning the lack of effect
of the films, including the men's previous indoctrination as civilians,
conflicting motivation, ineffectiveness of a single fifty-minute presentation when compared to years of exposure to influences of ordinary
life and the lack of a "sink-in" period.[93] A more empirical observation offered by an Information and Education Division officer himself
was that leadership is an all important factor in war, in any mass
movement. He believed that orientation perhaps failed in World War II
because the leaders themselves did not have serious convictions.[94]
Thus, still another concept, the two-step flow theory becomes a factor.

Thus, research on the "Why We Fight" series did indeed prove inconclusive. This may have been because of several reasons, including
inadequate tools of research. Specific factors may have been the
failure to ask the right questions or to prepare the films with
specific test objectives or items in mind. A personal interview with
A. A. Lumsdaine, one of the researchers, revealed that the research
group was called in to evaluate the series after the first four films
had been made. They found that no specific ofjectives had been set up
in the construction of the films, and thus they were forced to set up
objectives for the films on a secondhand after the fact basis.[95]

However, the films probably had more effect than the statistics
show. They may not, as the Research Branch showed, have changed opinions and attitudes or greatly affected motivation; but as tools for
reinforcement they were perhaps more effective. The "hypodermic needle"
theory of effect was still very prevalent at this time, with change
being the only criterion of the effectiveness of a persuasive message.

owever, in recent years the concept that reinforcement rather than
hange is the most probable effect of a persuasive message has been
:cepted.

Thus, looked at with hindsight, it appears that the films may
ave functioned very effectively as reinforcement agents, strengthening
inions already in agreement with those in the films.

These studies and others designed to cite the influence of films
military motivation point up the difficulty of modifying military
tivation within the American culture. As one study states, "Some
the evidence does indicate that films tend to reinforce motivations
ich are consistent with the milieu of daily life. . . . There is no
rrior cult in the U.S."[96]

Even if the films did fail in changing attitudes or increasing
tivation they should perhaps not be judged too harshly. They were
imarily information films and were created with this goal in mind.
so, as the experimenters themselves pointed out, it is perhaps
king too much for a single fifty-minute film to wipe out years of
fluence and predispositions.

FOOTNOTES - CHAPTER III

[1]77 Cong. Rec. 7074 (1941).

[2]Raymond D. Wiley, "Why We Fight: The Effort to Indoctrinate Personal Commitment in the American Soldier in World War II" (unpublishe seminar paper, Southern Illinois University, 1964), p. 2.

[3]Ibid., p. 3.

[4]Arch Oboler and Stephen Longstreet (eds.), Free World Theatre: Nineteen New Radio Plays (New York: Random House, 1944), p. 10.

[5]Cecil Brown, "Do You Know What You're Fighting," Colliers, 112 (December 11, 1943), 14.

[6]Francis Keppel, "Study of Information and Education Activities in World War II," manuscript, Information and Education Division Historical File, National Archives, Washington, D.C., p. 24.

[7]E. A. Steckel and K. E. Appel quoted in Wiley, p. 4.

[8]Keppel, p. 8.

[9]Ibid.

[10]Ibid.

[11]Ibid., p. 10.

[12]Ibid., p. 11.

[13]Ibid., p. 15.

[14]James Mock and Cedric Larson, "Public Relations of the U.S. Army," Public Opinion Quarterly, V (June, 1941), 279.

[15]Ibid., p. 280.

[16]Keppel, p. 15.

[17]Time, XXXVIII (August 18, 1941), 36.

[18]Ibid.

[19]George McMillan, "Government Publicity and the Impact of War," ublic Opinion Quarterly, V (Fall, 1941), 395.

[20]Keppel, p. 18.

[21]Ibid., p. 22.

[22]Ibid., p. 25.

[23]Ibid., p. 116.

[24]George Thompson, Dixie Harris, Pauline Oakes, and Dulany errett, The Signal Corps: The Test (Washington, D.C.: U.S. Government rinting Office, 1957), pp. 414-415.

[25]Ibid., p. 415.

[26]78 Cong. Rec. 674-676 (1943). Remarks of Gen.George Marshall.

[27]Thompson, Harris, Oakes and Terrett, p. 415.

[28]Richard MacCann, "Documentary Film and Democratic Government: n Administrative History from Pare Lorentz to John Huston" (unpublished h.D. dissertation, Harvard, 1951), p. 341.

[29]Richard Griffith, Frank Capra (London: The British Film nstitute, n.d.), p. 31.

[30]Thompson, Harris, Oakes and Terrett, p. 415.

[31]Colonel R. C. Barrett (Retired), private telephone interview eld at National Archives, Washington, D.C., February, 1967.

[32]Memorandum from General F. H. Osborn, National Archives, ashington, D.C., Frank Capra file.

[33]Keppel, p. 175.

[34]Ibid.

[35]C. I. Hovland, A. A. Lumsdaine, and F. D. Sheffield, Experiments n Mass Communication (New York: · John Wiley & Sons, Inc., 1965), p. 22.

[36]Ibid., p. 23.

[37]Ibid., p. 24.

[38]Prelude to War, Army Orientation Film #1, Bureau of Audio-isual Instruction, Madison, Wisconsin.

[39] Bill Davidson, "They Fight With Film," Yank Magazine (March 5, 1943), 21.

[40] Memorandum, Frank Capra to Lowell Mellet, May 1, 1942, National Archives, Washington, D.C., Frank Capra file.

[41] Ibid.

[42] Ibid.

[43] Ibid.

[44] Arthur Calder-Marshall, The Innocent Eye (London: W. H. Allen, 1963), p. 203.

[45] Ibid.

[46] Ibid.

[47] Thompson, Harris, Oakes and Terrett, p. 415.

[48] Ibid., pp. 415-416.

[49] Clarke, p. 176.

[50] Thompson, Harris, Oakes and Terrett, p. 415.

[51] Memorandum, Capra to Mellett, May 1, 1942.

[52] Paul Rotha, Sinclair Road, and Richard Griffith, Documentary Film (New York: Hastings House, 1963), pp. 319-320.

[53] Griffith, p. 5.

[54] Ibid.

[55] "Frank Capra," Current Biography (New York: H. W. Wilson Co., 1948), p. 43.

[56] Note, National Archives, Washington, D.C., Frank Capra file.

[57] Memorandum, National Archives, Washington, D.C., Frank Capra file.

[58] Clarke, p. 176.

[59] Memorandum, National Archives, Washington, D.C., Frank Capra file.

[60] Ibid.

[61] Ibid.

[62] Griffith, p. 31.

[63] Clarke, p. 176.

[64] Note, National Archives, Washington, D.C., Frank Capra file.

[65] MacCann, p. 347.

[66] Ibid.

[67] Thomas Brown, "Army Film Utilization," Business Screen, VII (1945), 83.

[68] "U.N. Central Training Film Committee, Motion Picture Title List," November 21, 1944, Film Section, Library of Congress, Washington, D.C.

[69] Clarke, p. 180.

[70] Thompson, Harris, Oakes and Terrett, p. 416.

[71] Paul Horgan, "The Measure of Army Films," Business Screen, VII (1945), 38.

[72] "U.S. Army Films go to Public," Film News, IV (November 3, 1943), 3.

[73] Clarke, p. 190.

[74] Ibid.

[75] MacCann, p. 297-98.

[76] Memorandum, National Archives, Washington, D.C., Frank Capra file.

[77] Ibid.

[78] The Film Daily Year Book, ed. by Jack Alicoate (Hollywood: The Film Daily, 1944), p. 81.

[79] "Frank Capra," Current Biography (New York: H. W. Wilson Co., 1948), p. 43.

[80] James Agee, Agee on Film, ed. by McDowell Obolensky (New York: McDowell Obolensky, Inc., 1958), p. 56.

[81] Ibid., pp. 56-57.

[82]Rotha, Road and Griffith, p. 289.

[83]Agee, pp. 40-41.

[84]Davidson, p. 20.

[85]Hovland, Lumsdaine and Sheffield, p. 13.

[86]Ibid.

[87]Ibid., pp. 24-25.

[88]Horgan, p. 39.

[89]Ibid.

[90]Hovland, Lumsdaine and Sheffield, p. 64.

[91]Ibid.

[92]Ibid.

[93]Ibid., pp. 65-72.

[94]Raymond Wiley, private interview at Southern Illinois University, Carbondale, Illinois, March, 1964.

[95]A. A. Lumsdaine, private interview at University of Wisconsin, Madison, Wisconsin, October 6, 1966.

[96]Charles Hoban and Edward B. Van Ormer, Instructional Film Research 1918-1950 (Report of the Instructional Film Research Program, The Pennsylvania State College, October, 1951), Chapter 5, p. 12.

CHAPTER IV

THEMES OF THE "WHY WE FIGHT" SERIES

INTRODUCTION

The seven films in the "Why We Fight" series are divided into two types according to basic theme and content. The first three, Prelude to War (1942), The Nazis Strike (1943) and Divide and Conquer (1943), and the last, War Comes to America (1945, set forth a general explanation of how World War II began. These films contrast the two world orders--Axis and Allied--with a major emphasis upon specific events leading toward war, including actual battle and campaign tactics, strategy and the results of war. The other three, The Battle of Britain (1943), The Battle of Russia (1943), and The Battle of China (1944), describe how each respective country became involved in the war, the battles and campaigns fought by these countries and the effects of war upon the people and land of each country. Emphasis in these "ally" pictures is on description of the people of the country and the common bonds that exist between the Allies. A distinct focus is placed on actual battles that occurred when these countries were attacked, with the idea of building the people up in terms of their courage and fighting ability.

The basic premise behind all the films was given best expression by Chief of Staff George Marshall in his introductory remarks to Prelude to War which have been stated previously.

Thus, the films had two major emphases. The first was upon facts and information designed to document the story of the war, how it began and how it was being fought. The second emphasis focused attention on those principles and purposes for which the United States and its allies were fighting. Within this second area nine distinct individual themes appeared. These are: (1) people, (2) religion, (3) children, (4) historical traditions, (5) hatred of war, (6) leaders, (7) slavery-machines, (8) courage and integrity of the Allies, (9) Allies bought time for world.

PRESENTATION OF THEMES

Explication

The emphasis upon information was perhaps the overriding characteristic of the series. This emphasis was used in presenting all the major themes of the series. Facts and information were not used merely to inform the viewer objectively, but were used as "proof" in a persuasive sense. There was rarely any information for information's sake in the films; rather, each fact, each event, each statistic was used with a definite and distinct persuasive purpose in mind.

This "proof" generally took two forms. On the one hand, information was used to document how the United States and its Allies got into the war, despite the fact they did not want war, and how they were faring against the Axis powers. Information was also used to depict, despite the many claims of the Axis powers, how they desired war; how they brought about World War II; how they were planning to conquer the world and how they were faring.

Factual Documentation

The first use can be seen quite clearly in all of the films. In Prelude to War, the theme that we wanted peace and security is depicted by a sequence of events including scenes of the 1921 Washington Disarmament Conference, the 1929 Kellogg-Briand Pact and statistics on how the United States destroyed sixty percent of her naval tonnage. All of this was designed to prove that we wanted peace. In War Comes to America, the explanation of the complicated and controversial pattern of the United States' slow involvement in the war, beginning with an increase in naval appropriations on through the arms embargo bill to the actual day of the Pearl Harbor attack, is constantly buttressed by a variety of means. The increase in naval appropriations is shown by the Committee meeting to discuss this increase, including one of the members identifying the Committee and its purpose. When the repeal of the arms embargo bill is discussed both exponents and proponents of the bill are shown actually stating their positions. Assistant Secretary of State Dean Acheson describes the process leading to the repeal of the bill. The Triparte Pact is explained by Assistant Secretary of State Berle. The emphasis is upon specific facts and information from respected sources.

Actual film of proceedings is shown whenever possible. In other words, the "fact" or "truth" of a particular piece of information is not left to chance. The film does not merely conclude that something happened or this is the way a certain act or event came about. Information is always employed to document the contention or statement.

The ultimate use of this technique occurred in <u>Divide and Conquer</u>, when a Colonel Clear spoke for almost four minutes explaining the details of the German breakthrough in France and the Low Countries. Complete with battle map, pointer and Disney animations, Colonel Clear documented in somewhat complicated fashion exactly what happened. Here, too, however, the information was not presented just for viewer edification. It was used to point out that French, British and other allied defenders did not retreat in panic; nor were they disloyal or cowardly. Rather, they had utilized the wrong strategy and were forced to "retire" to Dunkirk.

Statistics

An important element in the information emphasis was the use of statistics. The films abound in them. They are stated in the narration, printed in titles and drawn in animations. They are used to document broader themes.

In <u>The Battle of Britain</u>, great emphasis is placed upon documenting the odds the RAF faced and how they performed in the light of those odds. We see few "rounded off" figures here. The narrator states, "Goering launched 26 major attacks in 10 days to get command of the air, and lost 697 aircraft. The British lost 153." At another point the narrator states, "Between August 24, and September 5 [1940], 35 major attacks were launched. The Germans lost 562 planes, the British 219 and the British saved 132 pilots." Again the narrator, referring to an attack on September 15, states, "Inside a cube 60 miles long, 38 broad and from 5 to 6 miles high, 200 individual dog fights took place in 30 minutes. Of the 600 German bombers, 185 were shot down." In The Battle of Russia, the narrator documents the extent of the Nazi defeat with the information that the Nazis lost 5,090 planes, 9,190 tanks, 20,360 guns, 30,705 machine guns, 500,000 rifles, 17,000,000 shells, 128,000,000 cartridges and 1,193,525 men, including 800,000 dead. In Divide and Conquer, the narrator depicts the nature of the Nazi takeover of France by stating that three-fifths of the country was under military occupation, there was a tax of 400,000,000 francs a day and there were over 2,000,000 French prisoners of war. In Prelude to War, the published figures from the German budget from 1932 to 1938 are given to point out the extent of the Nazi preparation for war.

All of the films contain an abundance of material of this nature. These examples serve as illustrations of the conciseness and explicitness of the documentation and the purposes for which it was used.

Battle Documentation

Another use of information and concrete data in the films was to document a battle or campaign. Here, also, generalizations concerning how a battle was fought do not appear. Reference was already made to the example in Divide and Conquer where Colonel Clear spoke. The other films, while not utilizing a lecture approach, placed great emphasis upon battle strategy. This approach is again not just for the sake of informing the viewer. In the "ally" films the documentation of battle strategy is used to instill respect for the fighting ability and courage of the Allies. In The Battle of Britain, the

German strategy is outlined through the use of narration and Disney animations. The German strategy of "wedge and trap" is explained in detail with references to how well it worked in Poland, France and the Balkans. The Russian strategy of "defense-in-depth" is then explained; rather than meeting the Nazis on the border and being smashed and divided, the Russians gave up ground slowly and ultimately formed a solid wall of defense. In Divide and Conquer, detailed information is given regarding the French military strategy involving the Maginot Line. It is revealed that the French have seventy-eight divisions on the Belgian border, seventeen in the Maginot Line, ten on the German border and three and one-half as a safeguard against Spain. The plan involving the armies' swinging like a giant gate into Belgium where the German attack was expected to originate is also carefully explained.

In The Battle of Britain and The Battle of China, the German and Japanese battle plans are explained in detail. In The Battle of Britain, the viewer is asked to "Look at the Nazi plan." A carefully documented explanation of the three phases of the battle plan follows, utilizing actual footage of Hitler and his general staff looking over maps. In The Battle of China, the Japanese plan is documented through an explanation of the Tanaka Memorial. In this same film, the battle for Shanghai is explained with the preface, "To understand the fighting that followed we must know something of the city of Shanghai itself." A detailed analysis follows, including a review of the battle itself. This same emphasis is realized in The Nazis Strike, with a detailed exposition of how Hitler took Czechoslovakia through the Sudetanland tactic.

Again, examples of this particular use of information and data
re numerous throughout the films. These examples are utilized to
oint out the use to which the information is put and do not suggest
he extent of their use.

Quotations

A favorite technique used to document the nature of the enemy,
specially Germany, is the use of direct quotations from Axis leaders,
specially Hitler. In Divide and Conquer, extensive use is made of
quotes from a speech Hitler made on October 6, 1939, in which he made
he Low Countries specific promises to respect their neutrality.
ctual film of Hitler delivering the speech in the Reichstag is shown
although it should be noted that this footage was used in other
ituations in other films) with the translated quotes "supered" over.

Again, this information is not used in a neutral sense. The
quotes are used again after a sequence showing the destruction of one
f the countries referred to in the speech. Thus, Hitler's statements
re juxtaposed against a record of the action he said he would not
ake. The quotes are used to prove what Hitler and the Nazis are
ike. The obvious implication is: "Look, we didn't put words in his
outh--the facts speak for themselves. This is what Hitler said and
his is what he did."

The same technique is employed in The Nazis Strike, where a
itler quote is juxtaposed against his action in attacking Austria.
n Prelude to War, direct quotes are given in German, Italian and
apanese with a translation in English following. This is prefaced
y the narrator's statement that it is "an exact translation." Direct

quotes are used from Churchill in The Battle of Britain, from Madam

Chiang Kai-Shek in The Battle of China, Joseph Stalin in The Battle of

Russia and President Roosevelt in War Comes to America. The idea that

America did not want war is emphasized by FDR's "We Hate War" speech

showing Roosevelt actually delivering that portion of the speech con-

taining the well-known phrase.

Visual Documentation

Of course, the greatest impact the information and fact emphasis

had was through the use of actual footage compiled from newsreels,

documentaries and other "real" film sources, both Allied and Axis.

When quotes of Hitler, Churchill and FDR are used, they are usually

shown speaking. Whenever battle plans are discussed, some footage of

a general staff pouring over maps is shown.

Actual combat footage is used extensively. Occasionally, the

source of a shot will be referred to specifically, such as in The

Battle of China when the narrator states: "These scenes were photo-

graphed by an American missionary and smuggled out of China after the

rape of Nanking." In Divide and Conquer, the narrator states, "You

will notice that the assault engineer knows exactly where to put his

high explosive charge in order to destroy the blockhouse."

At other times, the footage is obviously not directly related to

the specific incident as a number of "stock" shots are repeated through-

out the films. Even though "stock" footage is employed the shots are a

record of reality. The use of production shots was kept to a minimum.

Occasionally, out-of-focus and other poor footage is included to

lend the aura of reality and "being there" to the events described.

The specific use and style of the footage will be discussed in
Chapter VI.

Other Uses

Innumerable other uses of information, facts and statistics
abound in the films. In Prelude to War, for example, a shot of the
tablet of the Ten Commandments is accompanied by directions in the
shooting script stating that an exact replica of the original should
be used so that it would be easily recognizable. In The Nazis Strike,
a great deal of film is devoted to an explanation of the Nazi theory
of Geopolitics including actual footage of Karl Harshafer, the chief
philosopher, going over maps and drawing on blackboards. Specific
dates are almost universally used where applicable. It was "at dawn,
April 9, 1949" that Denmark was occupied. The story of The Battle of
Britain is told in chronological order with battles and attacks documented and described date by date. This use goes so far as the
narrator stating in The Battle of Russia, "That's Russia. Or to be
correct, the Union of Soviet Socialist Republics."

Thus, through narration, visuals, film, titles and animation, an
emphasis upon information and facts is apparent. However, it was not
reality acting as neutral bits and pieces of information, but as proof
and documentation for virtually every major theme in the films.

Contrast

Another method of presenting themes was to contrast the two
world orders that were at war. This was especially apparent in Prelude
to War, The Nazis Strike, Divide and Conquer and War Comes to America.

The emphasis upon contrast basically functioned as a framework into which many themes were placed.

The prime example of this occurs in Prelude to War. The film is almost in the form of a three-way counterpoint among the Axis powers in turn contrasted to the free world. The theme of contrast, of two worlds opposing each other--and indeed, the idea of the film itself-- was based upon a speech given by Vice-President Wallace in 1942. Wallace spoke of a free world versus a slave world and the film carries the point home quite literally. "What are these two worlds of which Mr. Wallace spoke . . . the free . . . and the slave. Let's take the free world first." A drawing of two globes, one black and one white, accompanies the narration. As the narrator indicates the particular world, the camera zooms into that globe. This pattern of contrast is repeated twice in Prelude to War with the narrator stating, "That was the way of life . . . or better the way of death . . . in the other world. Now what of our world . . . the democratic world . . . what did we want, what did we do about it." Once again the camera zooms in on the white globe. War Comes to America utilized much the same method.

Even when contrast was not the basic structure of a film it was used constantly. In Divide and Conquer, the narrator depicts German preparedness for war by stating,"Six years of hard training and actual battle experience had made the German army look invincible. But what about the British and the French?" As was mentioned before, the basic style of Divide and Conquer is juxtaposing a quote by Hitler and scenes of the devastated country showing how the promise was broken. In The Battle of China, contrast is shown between what China and Japan took rom Western civilization. The narration constantly stresses that the

ar is a fight of "freedom against slavery" of "civilization against

arbarism," of "good against evil." In The Battle of Britain, the

fficiency and calculated methodology of the Nazi plan for conquering

ritain is contrasted with the fierce determination of the British

eople. In The Nazis Strike, the invasion of Poland is contrasted

ffectively through narration and actual combat footage with the

ritish and French leaders proclaiming "Peace in our time." In The

attle of Russia,the Nazi "wedge and trap" strategy is contrasted with

he Russian "defense in depth" strategy.

Thus, throughout the films, the method of contrast is employed

xtensively, especially the basic contrast between two world orders,

wo philosophies of life--between freedom and slavery.

THEMES

It is within these frameworks of explication and contrast that

ost of the themes of the films are placed. Within the structure of

he free world and the slave world several specific themes make them-

elves apparent. The free world is characterized almost universally

n terms of "the people." Children and religion also serve as major

hemes within this framework. The slave world is almost always depicted

n terms of specific leaders and their philosophies and statements,

ather than people. Within this world, consistent emphasis is also

laced upon slavery and antireligiousness.

Free World

The People

Within the framework of the free world is found the single most dominant theme in the entire series--the people. There is an almost mythical value and aura surrounding the concept of the people in the series. Part of this, at least in the first two or three films, can be traced to the director of the films, Frank Capra. Capra's films throughout the 1930's were almost without exception films about people, little people making it big, striking it rich, big people distributing wealth to the little people. Films such as Mr. Deeds Goes to Town, Mr. Smith Goes to Washington, You Can't Take It With You, and Meet John Doe are all examples of this emphasis upon the common man. Richard Griffith stated that Capra's films reflect the fantasy of good will. Indeed they do. The people are a vital and real force in Capra's films, usually fighting and overcoming some evil represented by big business, big government, and big money. The "good will" existed in the nature of the common people, the little man.

This is also true in the "Why We Fight" series. Without exception, the people are consistently referred to as being the backbone of the free world. References to "We, the people," "the common man," and "John Q. Public" abound. In Prelude to War, the narrator states, "John Q. Public still ran the country. Over here John Q. Public still read what he pleased." This was contrasted with scenes of book-burning in Germany. The consistent use of such phrases as "our way of living," "our entry into the war" and "we are fighting," point out this emphasis.

In Prelude to War, the freedom of the United States is symbolized through the words of great leaders with accompanying shots of statues of these men. The sequence ends significantly with a shot of the Lincoln Memorial showing the quote, "That government of the people, by the people, for the people . . . ," supered over as the narrator reads it. This, occurring early in the first film of the series, set the tone for subsequent characterization of the free world. Later in Prelude to War, the narrator states, "This isn't just a war, this is the common man's life and death struggle against those who would put him back into slavery. We lose it and we lose everything." In The Nazis Strike, "The people of Warsaw . . . had erected a wall of courage around their city." It was "not merely the British, but the British people who had declared war. . . ." In Divide and Conquer, the narrator, accompanied by visuals of people performing everyday tasks, states, "The people of these small neutral countries were peaceful, hard-working and free."

Even the great leaders of the free world, such as DeGaulle or Churchill, are closely tied both visually and orally to the people. Scenes of Churchill walking through the streets of London shaking hands with workers and DeGaulle being surrounded by French citizens as he takes his beaten army out of France clearly emphasize their closeness to the people.

In The Battle of Britain, the narrator states, "For something had happened here that Hitler could never understand. In a democracy it is not the government that makes war . . . it is the people." Further on the narrator states, over shots showing Britons working

at defending the island, "The people of Britain. The people who were
to be terrorized and forced to surrender. They knew the job they had
to do." Further examples of this theme in The Battle of Britain include the narrator stating, "A regimented people met an equally determined free people . . . and the regimented people quit . . . cold,"
and ". . . the war of the man in the street went on. He forgot what
it meant to have a night's sleep . . . But the people of London held
on . . . Chin up and thumbs up. They knew this was a people's war and
they were the people." Accompanying this are shots of people of
various ages and of both sexes performing many duties.

In The Battle of Russia, the "people of Leningrad" stopped Hitler.
"They seem very similar to the people of London . . . of Rotterdam . . .
of Warsaw." Further on the narrator concludes, "Yes . . . Here too
the legend of Nazi invincibility was shattered against the iron will
and courage of a determined people." Finally, in a repetition of the
theme used in The Battle of Britain, the narrator states, "There was
another item the Germans had overlooked. They overlooked people. And
generals may win campaigns but people win wars."

The Battle of China exhibits this same theme very explicitly.
Sun Yat Sen's establishment of a new order is illustrated by the fact
that he took "Government of the people, by the people, for the people"
as the theme for this new order. Numerous references to the people of
China fighting against Japan are evident, including, "and then it
happened--the will to resist by the Chinese people came forth and
unified the nation" and "The battle for Shanghai was a magnificent
victory for the people of China . . . the people who wouldn't surrender,

he people determined to fight for their freedom, their good earth . . .
he people who can't be beaten."

The "people" theme also received great emphasis in War Comes to
merica. Here the heritage of freedom is traced through statements of
eaders, ending with a shot of the Constitution as the narrator repeats
We the people" three times. The narrator concludes, "The people were
o rule, not some of the people, not the best people, or the worst, not
he rich people or the poor, but we the people, all the people." The
nited States is described by a long sequence depicting the nature of
he people. There is also a change in the narrator for the only time
n the series. The voice seems more "human" and less "unattached"
iving the sequence more of a "straight from the shoulder" appeal.
mphasis is placed on the "average man" depicting him as part of a
working people," "an inventive people," "a sports-loving people," "a
raveling people" and a "joining people." The word "we" is again
mphasized throughout the sequence.

This same idea was used in The Battle of Russia, The Battle of
hina and Prelude to War. Rarely are the German, Italian or Japanese
eople emphasized, described or referred to in any detail. In War
omes to America, the changing mood of the United States toward the war
s expressed not in terms of FDR or Congress, but through a Gallup Poll
otif with the narrator repeating "We, the people, had spoken."
ongress is always a "Congress, reflecting the voice of the people."
hus, throughout the films the "people" is the major theme and the
asic element by which the free world is identified.

Religion

Another theme of the free world is religion. It receives greatest emphasis in Prelude to War. The film describes the history of freedom by focusing on four great men of vision, all of them religious--Moses, Mohammed, Confucius and Christ. Each of their contributions is visualized and described. This is followed by a close-up of religious books on a shelf, including the Bible, Koran, and analects of Confucius, among others. The accompanying narrator states, "All believed that in the sight of God all men are created equal."

In Divide and Conquer, the narrator states, "The people of the democracies prayed for strength to meet the coming hour of terror," as the visual shows the interior of a church, and a priest blessing children. In The Nazis Strike, Marshall's statement supered over the figure of Christ on the Cross ends the film. In The Battle of Britain, film of London's greatest siege includes footage of St. Paul's Cathedral with the narrator stating, "But unscathed and triumphant stood the great cathedral of St. Paul's . . . a Christian monument defying barbarism." In The Battle of Russia, scenes of the Russian Archbishop in a church service are accompanied by the narrator stating, "And while in the churches of Russia men of God prayed for victory against the invaders . . . ."

All of these sequences attempt to establish the idea that religion is a mainstay of the free world as contrasted to the barbarism of the Axis powers. Little is said about the antireligiousness of the Axis powers except for one long dramatic sequence in Prelude to War, which established for the entire series the antireligious nature of the enemy, especially Germany.

The sequence begins with the depiction of the loss of traditional freedoms in Germany--speech, assembly, and free press. One by one these "obstacles" fall. "Finally there is only one obstacle left." This is accompanied by a long shot of a German cathedral. The film then cuts to a shot of the inside of a church with people kneeling and sunlight shining through a stained glass window. The music at this point is strongly religious. The camera then pans up to an inscription on the wall, "I am the light of the world. He that followeth me shall not walk in darkness." The camera continues to pan up to a shot of Christ in a stained glass window as the narrator states, "The word of God and the word of Fuhrers cannot be reconciled." A harsh voice then intercuts, "Then God must go." A rock crashes through the window to reveal a picture of Hitler on a building with "Heil Hitler" supered over. A voice depicting Albert Rosenberg then says, "Catholic and Protestant churches must vanish from the life of the people." This is followed by a montage depicting the erasure of religion by the Nazis, including shots of stormtroopers replacing a cross with a swastika, removing a plaque of the Ten Commandments with a hammer and a chisel, and of a ruined Catholic church with shattered statues and religious symbols on the floor. This sequence is followed by two voices representing Goebbels and Streicher saying, respectively, "Everything the Fuhrer utters is religion in the highest sense," and "Hitler is far too big a man to be compared with one so petty [Christ]." The closing shots of this powerful sequence show a picture of Hitler in shining armor on a white horse with school children singing "Hitler is our Lord . . ." while the narrator states, "Yes, take children from the faiths of their fathers and teach them the state is the only church, and the head of the state is the voice of God."

Thus, religion is not only depicted as a strong element of the free world, but is also shown being destroyed, crushed and replaced by the state in the Axis world.

It might be noted here that Frank Capra, a Catholic, was and is deeply religious. Elements of this religion were present in most of his feature films. Thus, it is not surprising that in this first film the strongly religious emphasis should appear. Also, Wallace's speech from which the main theme of the film came is strongly religious.

Children

Yet another theme of the free world was the emphasis on children, both as a positive "good" in the free world and as a target for death and injury in the slave world. In Prelude to War, the narrator describes an American: "And most of all he got a kick out of seeing his kids grow up." The film follows with a long tracking shot of Negro and white children singing in a choir. This same emphasis is seen in War Comes to America. The opening shot is a close-up of children pledging allegiance to the flag. A similar sequence in Prelude to War utilizes a montage of how we educate, raise and "in general, spoil our children." Following this sequence, German and Japanese children are shown drilling, and Italian children wear gas masks and participate in a war "game." This is contrasted with a montage of American kids at play. A quick wipe to a montage of German, Japanese and Italian children drilling is accompanied by the narrator, "Yes . . . while

their children were being trained to kill . . . John Q's kids were
giving pennies to help them have life."

In Divide and Conquer, The Battle of Russia, The Battle of
Britain and The Battle of China, the children theme was utilized on
the one hand to portray the brutality of the Nazis and on the other to
show how the people of the attacked countries cared for their children
and tried to save them. In Divide and Conquer, the narrator states,
over scenes of children being evacuated from a Paris railroad station,
"The despairing people of Paris sent their children south . . . praying
that some miracle would keep them from harm." The same scene is repeated in The Battle of Britain with shots of the people of London
sending their children out of the city. In The Battle of Russia,
Christmas, 1942, shows children at play, opening presents as the narrator states, "Just as in our home towns . . . it is the children's day
in Moscow."

Even more powerful, however, were scenes depicting Nazi and
Japanese brutality involving children. One particularly emotion laden
scene in The Battle of Russia shows piles of broken and twisted bodies
as the narrator states, "No . . . these aren't dolls . . . these are
children . . . mass murder by the orders of the high command." This
is followed by shots of "nerve shattered" girls as the narrator observes, "Young girls . . . but not young now . . . the attention of
the Nazi soldiers aged them quickly." In Divide and Conquer, shots of
injured children in a hospital in Belgium and refugee children in carts
and wagons accompany the narrator: "No school today, the sign says.
The children are otherwise occupied." Also in Divide and Conquer,

shots of emaciated French children accompany the narrator stating
that French children were growing up to the age of twelve without new
teeth. In The Battle of China, numerous shots, especially in the
battle of Shanghai, show Chinese women and men with dead and injured
babies in their arms. The same emphasis is used in the bombing of
London in The Battle of Britain, the siege of Leningrad in The Battle
of Russia and the siege of Warsaw in The Nazis Strike.

Scenes in all the films show dead and injured children--poignant
reminders, especially following shots of healthy, happy American
children, of what the slave world was like. This theme is somewhat
similar to the atrocity stories surrounding the German rape of Belgium
in World War I with one important difference. In the "Why We Fight"
series, as contrasted with most of the factual films of World War I,
visual proof was evident with both the truth and impact of the message
gaining considerably.

Historical Tradition

Another theme of the free and slave worlds was that the freedom
of the democracies and the Axis powers' ambition for world conquest
had deep historical roots. This emphasis upon historical tradition
was especially apparent in the explication framework.

Prelude to War begins with the question, "How did it [the free
world] become free? Only through a long and unceasing struggle inspired
by men of vision." This is followed by a long sequence depicting the
historical march of freedom. At first, the march encompasses a broad
world view through the work of such men as Moses, Mohammed, Confucius
and Christ.

Then it shifts to the United States and allied countries by emphasizing the Declaration of Independence and cutting in shots of monuments of such men as Washington, Jefferson, Garibaldi, Lafayette, Bolivar, Lincoln and others. The history then switches specifically to the United States with a montage of the great symbols of American freedom--the White House, the Capitol, the Washington Monument, the Tomb of the Unknown Soldier. This is accompanied by the narrator's quoting familiar phrases of freedom such as Lincoln's "Government of the people . . . ," and Patrick Henry's "Give me liberty or give me death."

The Nazis Strike utilizes the same historical theme in depicting Germany's historical ambition for world conquest. The sequence begins with a series of quotes in titles and signatures ("Bismarck, 1863," "Wilhelm, 1941," "Hitler, 1933") as the narrator states: "Germany's ambition for world conquest goes back a long way." The narrator concludes the sequence with "The symbols and the leaders change. But Germany's maniacal urge to impose its will on others continues from generation to generation." This is followed by a sequence documenting the last seventy-five years of German conquest and what it cost the world and Germany in terms of people killed and wounded and property lost.

The Battle of Russia emphasizes the historic will of the Russians to resist invaders. The sequence opens with a title "1704" and accompanying scenes showing how Russia turned back Sweden. The titles "1812" and "1914" are shown with appropriate footage portraying Russia's turning back invaders again. The sequence concludes with the narrator stating, "Yes . . . for 700 years the Russian people have had to fight to defend their land against would-be conquerors." The Battle of China also utilizes the history theme. In the beginning of the film the premise is established that China is history, land and people. In showing China's history, emphasis is placed upon the contribution China has made to world learning. The narrator states, "But more than four thousand years ago the Chinese Empire was already in existence. And more important, so was a Chinese civilization of art and learning and peace." The narrator concludes: "Well, in all their four thousand years of continuous history, they have never waged a war of conquest." This is followed by a sequence emphasizing what China has taken from Western civilization in more recent times, including universal school- ing, the Boy Scouts and freedom of religion, accompanied by scenes of Sun Yat Sen and the good elements he and the Chinese chose from Western civilization.

In War Comes to America, the historical heritage of democracy is depicted beginning with Jamestown in 1607 and the Pilgrims in 1620. It is emphasized that the Pilgrims came in search of "freedom" and estab- lished a colony of "free citizens." The sequence continues with the march of freedom culminating in a montage showing the U.S. Constitution and the four freedoms outlined in supered titles. This is followed by a depiction of the war we fought "in defense of this liberty." The titles "1775," "1812," and "1914" explode out of smoke followed by footage from commercial motion picture features depicting various battle scenes. Thus, the basic idea for which the United States fought--"all men are created equal"--and the concept of the United

States fighting now as it had fought throughout its history "for the future freedom for Americans" are dramatically emphasized.

We Hate War

Another major theme evident in the "Why We Fight" series is the concept that the United States and its allies did not want war. They fought defensively only because it was necessary. This is very evident in Prelude to War, when the narrator notes how we scrapped our army, navy and air force. The narrator states, "We let our hopes for peace become so strong that they grew into a determination not to fight unless directly attacked." Later on, the narrator makes it clear who the aggressor was when he states, "It was inevitable that these countries should gang up on us."

In Divide and Conquer, the peoples of the Low Countries are described as "peaceful, hard working . . . and free." Norway: "They hadn't wanted war. They had done everything to avoid it." France: "Hitler knew that the French had tried to avoid war instead of preparing for it. That knowledge was one of his greatest weapons." (Accompanying this were shots of the French Cabinet with "No more war" supered over and a treaty with "Kellogg-Briand Pact" supered over.) Holland: "Before Rotterdam knew it was at war, its outlying sections and airports were occupied." In The Battle of China, it is made clear that the Chinese, "in their 4,000 years of continuous history . . . have never waged a war of conquest. They are that sort of people." In the beginning of the picture the narrator states, "Why have the Chinese been forced to fight?" In The Battle of Russia, Stalin echoes this theme by stating,"The whole world is looking to you to destroy the German horde. The war you are fighting is a war of liberation . . . a just war." Russia is represented as wanting peace by showing Ambassador Litvinoff stating, at the League of Nations, "The state I represent entered the League with the sole purpose of the maintenance of individual peace."

The "we hate war" theme receives the greatest emphasis in reference to the United States in War Comes to America. Indeed, the very title of the film suggests the direction the war took. This title was no accident. The film was originally titled America Goes to War, but was changed to suggest that America did not in fact go to war, that war came to America. The wars the United States fought are characterized as "defenses of liberty," as "withstanding the challenge." War comes to the United States and it responds in a defensive manner. Further on the narrator states, "We hate war . . . we know that in war it is the common man who does the paying and the suffering and the dying. We bend over backwards to avoid it." The question is then asked, "Did we want war?" It is answered by showing that we fought the First World War to make the world safe for democracy and then scrapped much of our army, navy and air force through the Washington Disarmament Conference and the Kellogg-Briand Pact. Further emphasis is given by the narrator's stating that it was "to protect our shores" that the U.S. authorized the construction of a two-ocean navy. We also occupied bases in Greenland which "in our hands became bases of defense."

Slave World

The slave world is also very distinctly characterized. Some of this has been mentioned in reference to themes underlying the free world, such as antireligion and historical inheritance of the ambition for world conquest. However, two basic themes occur throughout the films which distinctly apply to the slave world in contrast to the free world.

Leaders

The first and most universal theme is that the Axis powers are almost always depicted in terms of leaders--in terms of specific individuals rather than a "people" as in the free world. The enemy thus becomes symbolized in terms of leaders. In Prelude to War, war began in Italy when "an ambitious rabble rouser" came into power. In Japan, war was caused by "a gang of Japanese" who took "advantage" of the people's worship of the emperor. In Germany, it was "the third gangster." The narrator states, "Take a good look at these humorous men. These were to be rulers of the ruling race."

Consistent reference is made to the leaders and their actions. The narrator states, "Think of the bread . . . the automobiles . . . the good things of life that the German, Italian and Japanese leaders might have given their people." The sequence closes on close-ups of Hitler, Mussolini and Hirohito as the narrator states, "Remember these faces, remember them well. If you ever meet them, don't hesitate." In The Nazis Strike, the history sequence depicting Germany's tradition of power and conquest is symbolized in terms of three leaders--Bismarck, Wilhelm and Hitler.

The narration also emphasizes this theme by denoting the action
of a single individual. For example: "Hitler had seen Hirohito grab
off Manchuria. He had watched Mussolini get away with the rape of
Ethiopia." In The Battle of Britain, the narrator states, "The one
obstacle that stood between him and world domination . . ." and ". . .
had given him more than one hundred million slaves." Further use of
this theme is found in Divide and Conquer: "Before striking with his
armies he used another weapon." "While Hitler was making these promises,
his generals were coldbloodedly picking out the first victim." "But he
couldn't take Norway . . . so he clubbed Norway into submission and got
what he wanted."

In Divide and Conquer, Hitler is likened to John Dillinger.
Further references to this theme include: "His next move must obviously
be through France . . . to get his southern claw." In The Battle of
China, the rape of Shanghai is a "nightmare of cruelty . . . all the
more horrible because it was deliberately planned by the Jap High
Command." In The Nazis Strike, the German people were forced to work,
forced to produce, or it was concentration camp or death for them. The
narrator states over a close-up of Himmler, "And this is the man who
gives it to you." Hitler and his cohorts were making Germans into
"unthinking, insensible weapons."

Whenever Germany planned an attack it was always symbolized by
Hitler, Goerring and/or some generals giving orders, looking at a map
and planning the campaign. When the Luftwaffe is sent against Britain,
it is Goerring who sends them, who is the symbol for them. When a
German victory is shown, it is Hitler who is pictured as happy. In

The Nazis Strike and War Comes to America, the takeover of Paris is
visualized by Hitler's riding through empty streets and standing on
the banks of the Seine. The same is true of the takeover of Vienna.
In The Battle of Russia, it was Hitler who had promised his generals
they would be in Moscow. A shot of captured German generals symbolizes
the entire German defeat.

When countries that fell to defeat without much of a fight are
referred to, such as France and Norway, the defeat was not because of
the people but because of a traitor or weak leader. Norway fell--
its guns were silent--not because of the cowardice of the people, but
because of Quisling. France's spirit was weakened by the ideas of
Maginot. The narrator states, "Between the ideas symbolized by these
two men [Foch and Maginot] may well lie the military story of the fall
of a great nation." In France it was Petain, "Old and tired and egged
on by men like Laval," who sold the country down the river. In The
Battle of Russia, Rumania fell because it was "governed by Young King
Michael, who was only a tool in the hands of Hitler's puppet, General
Anlensar." Bulgaria fell because it was "ruled by King Boris, always
a disciple of German imperialism." "All had sold their countries out
to Hitler. Now, threatened by a revolt of their people . . . they were
only too glad to be protected by Hitler's armies."

That this emphasis should occur is not surprising; only the
almost universal applicability of it is. It is a long recognized
concept of propaganda that it is easier to vent hatred and vengeance
on specific individuals than on a generalized country or people. The
people of the Axis powers were almost never described. If so, only

in the sense that they were forced to do something, or that advantage had been taken of them.

Slavery-Machines

The other theme by which the slave world was characterized was slavery--a mechanized, dehumanized force. In Prelude to War, the basic theme was that of a slave world opposed to a free world. This set the tone for the subsequent depiction of the Axis powers. In characterizing the conflict, the narrator in Prelude to War states, "This isn't just a war, this is the common man's struggle against those who would put him back into slavery." In referring to the Axis leaders, the narrator states, "All other people will be your slaves," and "What helpless people were they planning to bomb . . . slaughter . . . drive into slavery." In speaking of the German people themselves, the narrator in Prelude to War states, "They gave up their rights as individual human beings . . . and became part of a mass, a human herd." In The Nazis Strike, Hitler is quoted: "There will be a class of subject alien races. We need not hesitate to call them slaves."

Having set up the slave theme through Hitler's own words, the remaining films utilize the idea whenever countries were attacked or overrun by Hitler. In Divide and Conquer, it is: "By nightfall, Denmark is erased as a nation and the Danes go into slavery," and "2,000,000 French prisoners go to work as slaves." It is French civilians who "must slave on farms or in factories." In The Battle of Britain, the fall of Austria, Czechoslovakia, Poland and Denmark ". . . had given him more than one hundred million slaves." In The Battle of China, it is: "The struggle of freedom versus slavery" and

"Just as Russia was to be enslaved for German use . . . ." In The
Battle of Russia, the narrator states, "Nazi slavery didn't appeal to
them," and "Hitler needed more slave labor and more cannon fodder for
the attack on Russia." These are a few examples of the many uses of
the slavery theme to characterize the Axis powers.

The other motif in this characterization, although not as prominent as the slavery theme, was the Axis powers being likened to machines
and inhuman forces. In The Battle of China, the narrator states, "The
Japs were fighting more than the Chinese people. They were fighting
the Chinese land . . . these two were enemies that defied the Jap war
machine." In the same film Japan is depicted using Western civilization to create "one of the world's most powerful war machines." In
The Battle of Russia, Hitler needed Rumanian oil to "power his war
machine." In War Comes to America, it is "slaves for his industrial
machine."

The Nazis, especially, were characterized in impersonal terms.
Some of these included "the Nazi scourge," "the Nazi blitz," "the
trojan horse," "the jaws of the Nazi whale," "the Nazi steamroller,"
and "the coming hurricane of terror." General Marshall's quote ending
every "Why We Fight" film stated that victory could not be complete
without the "utter defeat of the war machines of Germany, Italy and
Japan." Thus, the Axis powers were often pictured as inhuman forces
let loose on the world to make slaves of the people of the free world.

The Allies

There were three "ally" films in the series. These films, The
Battle of Britain, The Battle of Russia and The Battle of China, had

several themes peculiar to them alone as well as having most of the general themes mentioned thus far.

Courage and Integrity of the Allies

The most dominant theme of these films was the emphasis upon the courage, integrity and fighting ability of the United States' allies. This theme is especially evident in The Battle of Russia. The opening sequence is composed of five quotes by Secretary of War Henry Stimson, Secretary of the Navy Frank Knox, Chief of Staff Marshall, General McArthur and President Roosevelt. The quotes are designed to build up the Russians as fighting allies. Typical of these quotes is this statement by Knox: "We and our Allies own and acknowledge an ever-lasting debt of gratitude to the Armies and the people of the Soviet Union." Another quote by President Roosevelt supered over scenes of retreating Germans emphasized the ability of the Russians: "On the European front the most important development of the past year has been the crushing offensive on the part of the great armies of Russia against the powerful German army."

The entire sequence of the battle of Leningrad emphasizes the courage of the Russian people. Shot after shot dramatically outlines the terrible hardships the people of Leningrad endured. The narrator accompanies it: "Bombs from the air couldn't force the defenders of Leningrad to surrender. Winter couldn't do it, hunger couldn't do it. Their determination never faltered." The narrator concludes this sequence with, "And now . . . the whole world spoke in admiration of the city of steel."

Sequence after sequence showing battles for individual Russian cities reiterated this theme. The Odessa battle is described as an "heroic siege," as having "held up the whole Nazi thrust into the Crimea." The destruction of Sevastopol is characterized by the narrator: "The Russians knew their cities would be demolished, but their objective was not to save cities but to destroy Germans."

A particularly gripping sequence tells the story of Russian guerrillas who, with "a minimum of glory and a maximum of determination," fought on. "Ahead of them lay nothing but the rope and the halter . . . but they stayed behind and went on fighting." Close-ups of Russian faces accompany the narrator. "Their grim faces told of their determination . . . to fight and to die . . . but never to surrender."

Russian fighting ability was built up by describing the Nazi "wedge and trap" strategy and the Russian "defense in depth" theory. Russian ability is shown by depicting how successful the Germans had been with this method in Poland, France and the Balkans and how the Russians did not fall into the trap by placing all their men on the border. Utilization of their cities to slow down the German Blitzkreig was also an example of their courage and skill.

Emphasis upon building up the "courage and fighting ability of the allies" also occurred in The Battle of China. Statements such as, "We are China's ally rather than they ours, because they have been fighting Japan for seven years," were designed specifically to encourage respect for China. The Burma Road sequence contributes greatly to this theme. It first of all sets up the problem as seeming to be impossible. Several "experts" stated it would take years to build such a road. Then it is shown how the Chinese built it in less than twelve months--"a monument to the new spirit of the new China."

As in The Battle of Russia, the courage of the Chinese people is shown throughout the film by scenes depicting the battle for cities, especially the battle of Chungking. This battle became "the symbol of their indestructible spirit." The film also defends losses which might reflect badly on the Chinese. The narrator states, "Out of our defeats, the Chinese lost the Burma Road. But still the Chinese courage never faltered . . . her determination never weakened. In the history of those long and tragic months of black defeat in 1942, one bright page stands forth . . . a page written by our Chinese allies."

The Battle of Britain demonstrated this theme by focusing specific attention on the RAF. "Those few men with wings . . . alone in the sky . . . were shooting down more than the Luftwaffe. They were smashing the whole Nazi plan of world conquest." The odds facing the RAF were carefully spelled out: "The RAF came . . . facing odds of six . . . eight . . . ten to one." The intelligence of the British fighters is emphasized by depicting how the planes of the RAF were scattered in fields and not grouped in bunches, as in Poland, to be smashed while on the ground.

The people of Britain are also used to illustrate this theme. "And underneath the war in the air the war of the man in the street went on. He forgot what it meant to have a night's sleep. He learned to exist with very little food . . . But the people of London held on . . . chin up and thumbs up." The idea is presented that the government

finally had to force the people to stop working because overfatigue
was hurting production. The bombing of Coventry and the mass burial
scenes that followed also illustrated the courage of the people. The
narrator states, "The people of Coventry dug their loved ones out of
the blasted ruins . . . saw them to their last resting place in a
common grave . . . and then turned without tears and without complaint
back to their lathes and their machines. Their jaws were set. Hitler
could kill them but damned if he could lick them." Later the narrator
concludes, "A nation that calls on cold courage when hot courage runs
thin may die, but it can't be defeated."

Allies Bought Time for the World

A theme closely connected with the previous one was that the
Allies not only saved themselves, but bought the world--specifically
the United States--time. The idea was emphasized that the Allies,
like us, were not just fighting for themselves, but for free men
everywhere.

In War Comes to America, the narrator states, "For if Britain
dies we would be in great peril." The British are characterized as
fighting for an idea, "an idea bigger than the country." In The Battle
of Britain this theme is emphasized over and over with such statements
as, "Crush that little island and its stubborn people and the world was
his," "Britain . . . the one obstacle that stood between him and world
domination." The idea that Britain's fall would be disastrous for the
United States is illustrated twice in the film by the same example:
the narrator states that if Hitler defeated Britain, "He would phone

his orders to Washington." Churchill's famous "never have so many owed so much to so few" line is presented near the end of the film, with the narrator stating in preface, "It was not only for the people of Britain, but the people of the world that Winston Churchill spoke when he said . . ." If any doubt remained concerning the explicitness of this theme, it should have been abolished by the narrator's final words in the film: "The RAF and people of Britain did more than fight to save England. They won for the world a year of precious time." In The Battle of Russia, Stalin speaks before a crowd while the narrator translates, "This war is being fought not only to eliminate the danger hanging over our heads, but to aid all people groaning under the yoke of Fascism." In The Battle of China, it is made clear that Japan would not stop at conquering China. "One fact was obvious. China was to be the giant back on which Japan would ride to world conquest." This fact is documented by quoting from the Tanaka Memorial, the Japanese plan for world conquest. That China was putting up a stiff fight is illustrated by the narrator's stating, "The giant Japan intended to ride to world conquest was proving to be a bucking bronco." Madame Chiang Kai-shek reiterates this theme at the end of the film, "We in China, like you, want a better world . . . not for ourselves alone, but for all mankind. . . ."

There were other minor elements in all the "ally" films, such as emphasis on the common bonds between the United States and the Allies, particularly China, but no other major themes were evident in the films.

SUMMARY AND CONCLUSIONS

These are the themes of the "Why We Fight" series. There was little that was new, different or unexpected. Except for the idea that we hate war and fought only because it was necessary, the same themes appeared in World War I films and in many commercial motion pictures. The themes reviewed here appeared in almost all of the films and the examples used represent, in most cases, only a small portion of the number contained in the films.

The themes were expressed primarily through the narration, although visuals and music also made a significant contribution. Indeed, those scenes revealing the brutality of war upon the civilian population--shots of dead children, men and women holding wounded, dying and dead children, mass burial scenes, people weeping--need little commentary. They revealed by the pure power of the shot the horror of war.

The themes were, in general, not subtle. They revealed their message clearly, concisely and repeatedly. A case can perhaps be made for overstatement and oversimplification, but never for lack of clarity or meaning. The "Why We Fight" films, as part of the general orientation program of the Army, incorporated as themes many of the basic goals of that program--a belief in democracy, confidence in the integrity and fighting ability of our allies, resentment against the enemy who have made it necessary for us to fight, among others. These goals were meant to be understood and accepted. The themes of the films in the "Why We Fight" series were, then, messages to be clearly understood and accepted by the men watching them. Thus, the themes

156

were simple, to the point and repeated. Informative and persuasive subtlety was a luxury the Army could not afford.

Regardless of all that can be said about them, the themes did represent the answers to the basic question of the entire series: "Why do we fight?" More about exactly how these themes were presented is the subject of the next two chapters.

CHAPTER V

SOUND

INTRODUCTION

This chapter is an analysis of the sound track of the "Why We Fight" series. The chapter is divided into three areas: (1) speech, (2) music, (3) natural sound effects. Speech consists of the narration and the speech of characters in the film; music consists of that music composed for the films specifically and "natural" music recorded with the visuals; natural sound effects consist of natural sounds such as the noise of war and the various sounds of crowds. Each of the sound track elements will be analyzed first according to its characteristics and secondly, according to its functions.

The research for this chapter entailed recording all of the sound tracks of the films. This enabled the researcher to listen to the sound track separately from the films and identify specific characteristics. The sound was then roughly aligned with the visual sequence on the shot analysis sheets. This aided in establishing audio-visual relationships. Each of the sound elements was listened to separately on both the recordings and when viewing the films. Thus, each film, except The Battle of China, and each recorded sound track was listened to specifically for each of the sound elements.

That the visual component of the "Why We Fight" series is the dominant and most important element in the communication of the message,

157

there is little doubt. However, as in most films, sound plays a vital,

if obviously secondary, role. As Leonardo Da Vinci stated:

> The eye, which is called the window of the soul, is
> the chief means whereby the understanding may most
> fully and abundantly appreciate the infinite works
> of nature; and the ear is second, inasmuch as it
> acquires its importance from the fact that it hears
> the things which the eye has seen.[1]

In other words, as a more recent film critic has stated, "The film is

not purely a visual medium. It has never been purely a visual medium."[2]

Breaking it down even further, Karel Reisz stated, "The compilation

film leans very heavily for its mood on what the commentator says, on

the inflection of his voice, and the pace of his delivery."[3]

Thus, although it is by nature a secondary element in the film

medium, sound does play an important part in the communication of the

message. It is the purpose of this chapter to analyze that part.

SPEECH

Of the three basic sound elements in the "Why We Fight" series,

speech, particularly the narration, is the most important. Not only

is it dominant in a strictly quantitative sense, it also performs the

greatest interpretive and communicative role.

Narration

Characteristics

Hugh Baddeley, in his book The Technique of Documentary Film

Production, states that narration in a documentary film should never

exceed two-thirds the total running time of the film.[4] While this

may be somewhat arbitrary and inflexible, it does provide some guide-

lines for measuring the narration in a quantitative sense. Based on this formula, the narration in the "Why We Fight" films, with the exception of The Battle of Russia and The Battle of China, falls under this maximum.

The following table provides the percentage of time out of the total film time in which there is narration.

Prelude to War	64%
The Nazis Strike	58%
Divide and Conquer	56%
The Battle of Britain	61%
The Battle of Russia	75%
The Battle of China	71%
War Comes to America	60%

The difference between The Battle of China and The Battle of Russia and the other films can perhaps be accounted for by the fact that the battles for Russia and China, as well as the countries themselves, were not as well known to the American soldier as the battles for Britain or Europe. Also, the battles for these countries were lengthy, involving several campaigns and many individual battles. In addition, there were somewhat complicated political issues to consider--especially with China--which required a great deal of explanation. Lastly, extensive film footage for these battles was not available as it was for the battles for Britain or France. All of these circumstances combined to produce a greater reliance on explanation and description through narration rather than visuals.

The narration in the majority of the films runs under the two-thirds limit. The films, however, seemed wordy and verbose, at least

in certain portions. James Agee stated in reference to <u>Prelude to War</u>,
"The method is more verbose than I wish it were or am sure it need be."[5]
In reference to <u>The Battle of Russia</u>, Agee commented, "<u>The Battle of</u>
<u>Russia</u>, next to <u>Desert Victory</u>, is the best film of the year. But,
like the other orientation films, it is saturated with words."[6] This
apparent verbosity can be attributed to two things: (1) certain lengthy
sequences where the narration goes on continuously, and (2) the narration
"interrupting" a sequence a number of times, which seems to be adequately
sustained by visuals. Lengthy,narration-filled sequence are often alter-
nated with ones where the narration functions merely to introduce a
scene, or at times, punctuate it. However, these instances are compara-
tively few and the lengthy descriptions and "unnecessary interruptions"
tend to dominate. For example, in <u>The Battle of Russia</u>, the idea is
presented that the fighting for Stalingrad went on into the night. The
visuals communicated this idea very well, but the narration was allowed
to intrude, stating that it was night and the battle raged on. Again,
in <u>The Battle of Russia</u>, the idea is communicated that Russia won despite overwhelming adversities. To get this idea across, the narrator
repeats "despite" six times.

> Despite the fact that Hitler's armies swept deeper
> and deeper into the Soviet Union and, by October
> 15th, stood practically within the shadow of the
> Kremlin . . .
>
> Despite the fact that the Soviet Government . . .
> and all foreign missions . . . were forced to move
> to Kuibyshev, 700 miles to the east . . .
>
> Despite Hitler's triumphant pronouncement "I can
> say that this enemy is already broken and will
> never rise again" . . .

Despite the fact that, by December, five hundred
thousand square miles of Russian territory . . .
and area equal to the entire middle western United
States . . . had fallen to the invaders.

Yes . . . despite Russia's loss of her best agri-
cultural areas . . . her most thoroughly developed
industrial plants . . . millions of her people . . .
thousands of tanks and planes . . .

Despite everything, these six weeks had lengthened
into nearly six months . . . and the dread Nazi
blitz had spluttered . . . stumbled . . . and
finally died.

The communication of this one idea takes one minute and thirty seconds
of straight narration.

The Nazis Strike contains a long explanation of the German theory
of geopolitics, which is almost completely sustained by a complicated
narrative explanation. Also, in The Nazis Strike, the narrator continually makes reference to "Scenes like these . . . ," "Where do you
think this is?" and "This is . . . ." The visuals can and do communicate the message in most instances. The narration becomes not only
superfluous, but also may be irritating. In The Battle of China, the
great westward trek of the Chinese people is presented with a narration
which seems at times unnecessarily overdramatic. The mere sight of tens
of thousands of people carrying the material of entire cities on their
backs accompanied by a powerful musical score conveys the drama by
itself. Sentences like, "The Chinese had other tricks to pull from
their patched and faded sleeves," or "Rail by rail, tie by tie, they
moved the great railroads across the vast country," become wordy, and
the power of the sequence seems lost through narrative oversatiation.
In The Battle of Britain, the same pattern emerges. The narrator at

one point states, "And here comes the Luftwaffe," when it is patently obvious that the Luftwaffe is coming.

Another device which strains the satiation point is the narrator's reading a title as it is shown on the screen. This occurs in every film in the series with regularity, but most frequently in War Comes to America. Throughout a Gallup Poll sequence the question being asked is not only shown on the screen, but recited by the narrator as well. Throughout the film such titles as "March, 1938" and April, 1939" are not only shown, but read as well.

Thus, throughout the films, although not overdone in a quantitative sense, the narration probably seems overbearing, superfluous and at times burdensome according to today's more sophisticated standards. However, this evaluation is based on this researcher's personal reaction. It must be remembered that the audience for which these films were made was not highly educated (sixty-three percent had gone to high school or college) and some were even illiterate.

Narrator Style. Walter Huston and Anthony Veiller were the two main narrators for all the "Why We Fight" films. Other "voices" would intercut at times translating a German, Italian or Japanese quote, with a heavy accent. However, Huston and Veiller carried the bulk of the narration. Only in The Battle of Britain and War Comes to America does a different voice function as narrator.

Huston's voice is older and somewhat raspy. His style is semi-dramatic, even-paced and definitely low key. It is a fairly heavy voice, filled with authority. Huston narrates most of every film except The Battle of China and The Battle of Britain.

Anthony Veiller's voice is high-pitched and more "biting" in quality than Huston's. He is most often used when a film takes on a definite instructional tone. He has a fairly dry, matter-of-fact delivery suited to material of a more descriptive and informative nature. Veiller's voice is more insistent and driving than Huston's. He is not as low key, yet he is never as dramatic or authoritative. He narrates part of every film, including all of The Battle of China.

The other two voices are used in The Battle of Britain and War Comes to America. In The Battle of Britain, we find the standard deep-voiced "voice of God" narrator. His voice is very dramatic with rolling tones and pointed inflection. It tends to be overbearing and over-dramatic, sounding at times like the announcer for "The Lone Ranger." In most cases, the shots and their construction accompanied by music and natural sound effects are dramatic enough. The addition of his voice makes a number of scenes heavy and slightly ridiculous.

The other narrator appears in War Comes to America. Here, Lloyd Nolan narrates a long passage describing the American people. The shift in narrator is an obvious attempt to achieve a "straight from the shoulder" approach. Previously, Huston is identified as a detached narrator, observing, but not participating. Nolan comes in with "Well, we are . . . ." He is one of the people being described, one of the boys. The change is effective.

Narration Styles. Hugh Baddeley states: "Commentaries that read like literature rarely sound well to an audience. . . . Some of the most effective are often slightly colloquial and tending towards the conversational in style."[7] For the most part, the narration in the

series attempted a colloquial-conversational style. It did not always
succeed, especially in the long descriptive passages in The Battle of
Russia and The Battle of China. Rarely did the narration, however,
attempt a literary or poetic style, such as is found in Lorentz's The
River. In Prelude to War, there are repeated references to a "Mr. John Q
Public." Although James Agee found them embarrassing because he felt they
betrayed an underestimation of the audience, they were definitely colloquial. A consistent attempt to couch ideas in ordinary language, including slang, is evident throughout the films. In Prelude to War, the
Axis powers are described as "all hopped up with the same ideas."
Mussolini "played all these ends against the middle." The narrator
states in reference to the new order in Japan, "No matter how you slice
it, it was still good old-fashioned imperialism." Mussolini "beat his
chest like Tarzan" and was consistently referred to as a "stooge." In
summing up Prelude to War, the narrator states, "The chips are down.
That's what's at stake." In Divide and Conquer, France was "ready to
be plucked," and when the German breakthrough came, "There went the old
ball game for France." In War Comes to America, the German military
budget for 1932 to 1938 made ours "look like peanuts." In The Battle
of Russia, ". . . the people of the Soviet Union knew they were on the
winning team." In The Nazis Strike, Hitler "found some stooges who fell
for this bunk." Mussolini was characterized as a "bush-league Fuhrer."
It looked as if the Japanese "were going to have a walkover" in The
Battle of China, but they "took a crack at Shanghai," then "hastily
called that deal off." In The Battle of Britain, "The preliminaries
were over. It was time for the main event." Later on, "The pace was

too hot. Something had gone haywire. The Nazis had to call time out."
Hitler "put Goerring on the hot seat" for not knocking the RAF out of
the sky.

Throughout the films, this colloquial, conversational, even
slangy style dominated. As one of the "Why We Fight" films itself
pointed out, 63% of the troops in this war had gone to high school or
college as compared to 20% in World War I. This figure shows improve-
ment. However, it also shows that over one-third of the troops did
not have a high school education. Thus, the need for an easy-to-
understand, common style of narration. The style made ideas and
information easier to understand. It also spoke to the men on their
own terms, in their own language. There was little of the deep-voiced
narrator rolling off polysyllabic words. This was a narrator that
talked the language of the G.I. It made concepts and ideas more
understandable and the films more realistic.

Relationship with the Visual. Another characteristic quality
of the narration is that it rarely existed independent of the visual.
As Hovland, Lumsdaine and Sheffield state, "The narration told the
story of the war and explained the scenes."[8] The narration did this
and more. It set the pace for most of the long descriptive sequences.
Whenever a film utilized a long explanatory or descriptive sequence,
the visuals duplicated the commentary. Thus, the visual pace was often
dependent on the pace of the narrator. In The Battle of Russia, while
the narrator states that food, fuel and grain are being transported to
the survivors of Leningrad, the visuals show a truck loaded with food,
a truck loaded with fuel and a truck loaded with grain, all coinciding

exactly with the pace of the narrator. When the narrator mentions there are 93,000,000 people in the Soviet Union, the title "93,000,000" is shown. When the narrator mentions 213,000,000 barrels of oil are produced each year in the Soviet Union, this figure is shown. In The Battle of China, the narrator frequently describes and refers to visuals with such comments as, "This is the Gobi Desert" or "This is Shanghai." In films such as The Battle of China and The Battle of Russia, this degree of duplication may have been necessary because of the basic unfamiliarity of the subject material. This is often looked upon as unnecessary by modern standards. However, the exact duplication of titles both visually and orally was made necessary by the nature of the audience. Examples of this duplication abound in the films. In Prelude to War, as the narrator refers in passing to the Axis powers' houses of government (the Reichstag, the Diet and the House of Deputys), the visual cuts to a shot of the outside of each building. The same is true when the narrator talks about a "farm boy in Iowa, or a bus driver in London or a waiter in a Paris cafe" not being concerned about "a mud-hut in Manchuria"; shots of an Iowa farm boy, a London bus driver, a Paris waiter and mud-hut in Manchuria coincide exactly with the narration. In War Comes to America, in attempting to make the dates and events preceding the war relevant, the narrator states, "While you were graduating from high school . . ." intercut with shots of Japan attacking Manchuria. The method aims at clarification and most likely achieves it. There is exact visual duplication of every statement. When the narrator states, "While you were playing sand-lot baseball . . . ," a staged production shot of boys playing baseball is shown.

he same process is followed through the sequence of graduation, first
ate, and running around in jalopies. This seems to slow the films
own. However, some sacrifice in visual flow was perhaps needed in
rder to ensure the communication of the ideas in the films.

Thus, in all the films' descriptive and explanatory scenes, the
isuals are tied to the narration. Neither has an independent existence.
his seems to hamper the flow of the films and make them rather static.
owever, one of the primary goals of the films was to convey informa-
ion. Thus, some degree of subtlety was necessarily sacrificed to the
reater needs of time and the necessity of appealing to great masses
f men.

Punctuation. The last characteristic of the narration was its
unctuation of the films. The concept of sound punctuating a film is
ot new or revolutionary. Roger Manvell, well-known British film
ritic, has observed that sound can be both realistic and functional.[9]
unctional sound can point, underline, link and emphasize the action.
n the "Why We Fight" series, the narration punctuates the film in two
ays. The most common form is the narration introducing a scene and
hen letting the visuals complete the message. This introductory
unction can be in the form of a paragraph as in The Battle of China,
hen the narrator states, in preface to the bombing of Shanghai, "To
nderstand the fighting that followed we must know something about the
ity of Shanghai itself." It can be a sentence, such as "At dawn on
eptember 1, 1939, Germany rolled into Poland." It can be a phrase,
uch as "2:00 P.M.," prefacing the events at Pearl Harbor. Often an
ncomplete sentence is used such as, "As we here in America observed

Good Friday . . ." In all of these instances, the narration sets the scene.

A second form of punctuation is the transition. Here, the narration often provides the link between different events. In Prelude to War, the question is asked, "Why are we at war? Is it because of Pearl Harbor . . . Britain . . . France . . . Poland . . .?" The narrator continues with the names of countries interspersed with shots of the war in these countries. In The Battle of Russia, the narrator describes the people of Russia by stating just the names of the people. This provides a concise and definite link and acts as a verbal cut to complement the visual. Thus, the narration often links sequences and in effect replaces the dissolve and/or fade which usually accompanies such a transition.

Natural Speech

The other form of speech consists of dialogue or the voices of people speaking alone.

Very little actual dialogue is used in the films. Few shots were produced for the films, thus eliminating a great deal of produced dialogue. It is also difficult to get dialogue when ducking bullets and shrapnel. The Battle of Britain contains almost all of the dialogue used in the entire series. Included are scenes in an air raid shelter, scenes involving two men caught in an air raid, two air raid wardens and an old couple entering their bomb shattered home. These scenes are all production shots and seem to stand out in the film as slightly false--at least foreign--because of the dialogue and quality of the pictures.

People speaking alone are prevalent in all films, especially
ar Comes to America. There are several scenes of FDR speaking, as
ell as Hitler, Mussolini and other Allied and Axis leaders. This
aterial was, of course, originally in another context and not created
or the "Why We Fight" series. Other films include scenes of the
apanese ambassador at the League of Nations, Haile Selassie asking
he League for aid, Winston Churchill speaking to the British people,
DR delivering a speech and Edward R. Murrow speaking over the radio.

However, the greatest use of a single person speaking is in
aterial created for the series. In Divide and Conquer, Colonel Clear
peaks for three minutes and fifty seconds. In The Battle of China,
olonel William Taylor describes the air war over China. In War Comes
o America, Assistant Secretary of State Acheson and Berle talk about
he progress of the war.

unction

Narration in the "Why We Fight" series has a two-fold function:
1) to impress, and (2) to instruct. The first function was the least
sed. Only infrequently did the narration make a conscious attempt to
mpress. There is none of the poetic quality of The River or the
riving forcefulness of "The March of Time." The impressiveness of
he narration comes mainly from low key comments and understatements
hich follow particularly dramatic passages. The narration also serves
o build up the tension or excitement of a passage through short, sparse
omments inserted into the flow of a sequence.

Impress. The first use can be seen quite clearly in The Nazis
Strike. Over scenes of Polish suffering, the narrator simply states,
"These things the Poles will not forget." This particular method is
used extensively in Divide and Conquer to depict the Nazi invasion of
the Low Countries. In The Battle of Britain, the burying of English
dead killed in Coventry, is followed by, "Hitler might kill them, but
damned if he could lick them." Prelude to War ends with,

> We lose it [the war] and we lose everything, our
> honor, the jobs we work at, the books we read, the
> very food we eat, the hopes we have for our kids,
> the kids themselves.

These passages are not shouted. They are presented forcefully and
quietly. In The Battle of China, the long march westward utilizes a
fairly impressive, though seemingly overdramatic narrative, stating
how the Chinese had picked up their country on their backs and transported it west. In War Comes to America, the beginning of freedom in
the United States is dramatically underlined by repetition of the phrase
"We, the people." Although examples such as this are evident in all the
films, they do not constitute a major function of the narration.

The narration also builds up tension and excitement in a sequence.
This is usually done by intercutting short sentences or words into a
long sequence. The prime example of this is in War Comes to America.
The narrator relates the events on December 7, 1941, by describing the
Japanese envoys' actions in Washington, then cuts to "Meanwhile, the
Japanese fleet . . . ." Later, the actual bombing at Pearl Harbor is
contrasted with the Japanese envoys' action in Washington, D.C. The
cuts between Washington and Pearl Harbor become shorter and shorter.
The narrator finally states just the time: "1:30 P.M.," "2:00 P.M.,"

"2:30 P.M. . . ." This simple method of lessening the narration to just the time of day effectively builds up tension and excitement. In The Battle of Russia, the simply stating of names of towns recaptured by the Russians as Russian soldiers march through them is another example of this function. This technique, used in all the films, builds up tension by combining narration, visuals, music and natural sound into an integral whole. The narration blends with the other filmic elements. It does not stand out either through quantity or quality.

Instruct. The second major function of narration is instruction. This is, by far, its biggest job. This function also receives the bulk of the criticism from Agee. When the narration explains and describes, it begins to bog down. At times it becomes verbose, complicated and difficult to understand. In War Comes to America, the narrator very carefully spells out the question being asked by the Gallup Poll and then proceeds with equal care to spell out the answer to the question. Divide and Conquer almost qualifies as a training film because of the predominance of instructional narration. The film basically consists of the description of battle plans and strategies. In The Battle of Russia, the Nazi theory of "wedge and trap" and the Russian plan of defense in depth are described in detail. Here, too, the narration dominates and the film seems to slow down. Much of the instruction in the films arises from these descriptions and explanations of battle plans and strategy. They vary in length from twenty seconds to Divide and Conquer's three minute and fifty second sequence. They are almost always accompanied by a Disney animation which illustrates the narration, but is rarely able to alleviate the seemingly static and

word-saturated nature of the scene. In <u>The Battle of Russia</u> and <u>The</u>
<u>Battle of China</u>, a great deal of time is spent in carefully describing
the respective countries in terms of their history, land and people.
Great use is made of specific names, dates and places. A great deal
of information is imparted, but seemingly at the loss of filmic flow.
The concept of historical tradition in both the free and Axis powers
is an important theme which requires a great deal of narration. Every
film with the exception of <u>The Battle of Britain</u> utilizes narration for
this purpose. In <u>The Nazis Strike</u>, a relatively long scene describes
the history of German aggression from Bismarck to Hitler. In <u>War Comes</u>
<u>to America</u>,the historical march of freedom in the United States also
employs a great amount of narration.

Another source of instructional narration is when a plan or
theory is discussed. In <u>The Battle of China</u>, the Tanaka Memorial,
Japan's plan for world conquest, is explained in detail. The narration, by necessity, must and does carry the burden of the message.
<u>The Nazis Strike</u> contains a long complicated discussion of the German
theory of geopolitics. Here again the narration carries the bulk of
the message. In all the films the necessity to explain and carefully
document statements arising out of the strong emphasis on facts and
information, requires a great deal of narration. The narration is
necessary, but at times it results in overdrawn and lengthy scenes.
At times great detail and information is communicated which seemingly
adds little to the basic explanation. The emphasis upon positive
proof and clearness, however, often necessitated too much information
rather than too little.

Variety. Natural voices are used to create variety. The same
wo narrators verbally document almost all of the films creating a
istinct lack of vocal variety. This problem is alleviated by scenes
f people actually talking. Rather than the narrator stating what FDR
aid in a speech, it is better from a variety standpoint to hear and
f possible see FDR make the statement. This technique is used in all
he films. In The Battle of China, Madame Chiang Kai-shek states that
hina is fighting not only for herself, but for the whole world.
hurchill, in The Battle of Britain, speaks several times. In War
omes to America and Prelude to War, FDR is heard several times. In
he Nazis Strike and Divide and Conquer, Hitler and Mussolini speak
ften. The most effective use of voices to add variety is in War Comes
o America. Radio commentators such as Edward R. Murrow, H. V. Kalten-
orn and William L. Shirer are used several times to convey information
hich could have been given by the narrator. Divide and Conquer's
cene involving Colonel Clear is another attempt to add variety. The
ilms have an inherent variety in the visuals, but the narration can
nd does become at times monotonous. The addition of natural sounds
nd voices to complement the visuals adds variety to the sound track
nd the films as a whole.

NATURAL SOUNDS

The "Why We Fight" series makes great use of a variety of natural
ounds. They are used to perform several distinct functions and are an
mportant part of the sound track.

Characteristics

Sound of War

The most dominant form of natural sound in the films is not really a "sound." It is a combination of many individual sounds which form the sound of war. Included, among others, are explosions, bombs dropping, airplanes diving and guns firing. All of these blend together, are intercut, and at times juxtaposed to form an audio image of war. This sound is used extensively in every film, but receives special emphasis in The Battle of China and The Nazis Strike with their concentration on Axis destruction of cities.

Voice

A second type of natural sound is the human voice. We are not referring to a voice speaking alone or dialogue. Voice, in this sense, means the "noise" of a crowd. The voices of crowds are especially prevalent in German, Italian and Japanese mobs. In War Comes to America a newspaper hawker is seen yelling, "Italy attacks Albania." In The Battle of Russia, Russian guerillas recite an oath. Crowd noises are prevalent in all the films, but especially in Prelude to War. Here, the sounds of Japanese mobs yelling "Banzai," Italians screaming "Duce" and German hordes shouting "Sieg Heil" form much of the impact of the film.

There are, of course, a variety of other natural sounds which contribute to the films in a number of ways. They are for the most part of a singular and infrequent nature. Naming all the various sounds such as bells, motors, etc., would be tedious and serve no purpose.

unction

Natural sound effects perform three basic functions in the "Why
'e Fight" films. They are to: (1) punctuate, (2) create reality, and
3) create atmosphere.

unctuation

The sounds of war, most frequently explosions, often punctuate
nd accent the films. In <u>Divide and Conquer</u>, explosions act as an
ttention-getting device preceding the names of countries attacked by
ermany. In <u>Prelude to War</u>, the narrator states,"Was it because of
explosion] Pearl Harbor?" In <u>The Nazis Strike</u>, explosions precede the
ord "War" in the narration, creating the same attention-getting factor.
n <u>The Battle of China</u>, an explosion acts as a verbal cut and exclama-
ion point when it follows "Now a great change has taken place." Ex-
losions are used in <u>War Comes to America</u> to provide transitions between
ewspaper headlines showing U.S. ships being torpedoed. All of the
ilms utilize explosions to punctuate.

eality

A second use of natural sounds is to create reality and to lend
uthenticity and credence to scenes and sequences. Facts and informa-
ion used as proof for many of the concepts put forth are often empha-
ized. Natural sounds, coupled with the visuals, contribute greatly to
he reality of the information. The sounds of war lend reality to the
ilms; the sound of guns firing, bombs exploding and planes diving
lend together with the visuals to create the reality of war and
estruction. The natural sounds at times dominate a scene. Often,

much of the impact of the air battles over England is caused by the sounds of planes diving, bombs falling and guns firing.

Atmosphere

The last function natural sounds perform in the "Why We Fight" films is the creation of atmosphere. The narrator often introduces a scene involving fighting and then withdraws to let natural sounds carry the message creating the atmosphere of war and destruction. In Prelude to War, the narrator asks what are we fighting for--is it because of Pearl Harbor, Britain, France, Poland, . . .? Between the names of the countries mentioned, natural sounds along with visuals create an image of war. The same method is employed in all the films, including the destruction of Nanking in The Battle of China, the bombing of Coventry in The Battle of Britain, the siege of Warsaw in The Nazis Strike, the siege of Stalingrad and Leningrad in The Battle of Russia and the Pearl Harbor attack in War Comes to America. The narrator sets the scene and lets the visuals and sound take over. There is usually no music or further narration in these scenes. Thus, the sounds of war create the image of war. This atmosphere is so distinct and overwhelming that it is apparent without the narrator.

In summary, natural sounds perform many important functions in the "Why We Fight" films. In many instances they carry the message of the films almost by themselves. Thus, natural sounds are not used merely to duplicate the visuals but are used "plastically." They are manipulated and used to perform very distinct functions.

MUSIC

Music is the third and last element of the sound track to be
onsidered. In some ways it is the least effective element. The
usic was composed by well-known film composer (Lost Horizon, Meet
ohn Doe), Dimitri Tiomkin and played by the Air Force Orchestra.

orm

ull Orchestra

The music in the "Why We Fight" series generally takes five forms.
he first, and by far the most prevalent, is the full orchestra. This
orm is found in all the films behind every type of scene. It performs
number of functions which will be discussed later in the chapter.

inging Chorus

The second most prominent form of music is the singing chorus.
his form is used extensively in The Battle of Russia to suggest the
ature of the people. It is also used throughout the other films to
onvey emotion which the other forms of music could not effectively
ortray. In War Comes to America, a chorus sings "My Country 'Tis of
hee" as an animated map depicts the growth of the United States. In
he Battle of Britain, a chorus sings "Onward Christian Soldiers" under
urchill's voice. The film ends with the RAF chorus singing "There
ll Always Be an England." In The Battle of China, a chorus sings
der the westward trek sequence, adding emotion to the scene. In all
ese examples a chorus with orchestral accompaniment creates variety
d more effectively reflects the nature of the scene.

178

Brass Band

The third form of music is the brass band. This is often syn-
chronized with visuals of a marching band. It is used in Prelude to
War and War Comes to America. Other than these two films, however,
the form is not used.

Solo Instrument

The fourth type of music is the solo instrument. Almost without
exception, this consists of a bugle or a drum. The bugle call opens
and ends each "Why We Fight" film, acting as an attention-getter and
lending an immediate military flavor to the films. The drum beat is
most often used under narration to depict the growth of a movement, a
march on another country or preparation for war. Other than these two
instances there are no other solo instruments used in the series.

Solo Voice

The fifth and final form of music used in the films is the solo
voice. This form is used once, in War Comes to America. It is a
woman's voice singing "The Last Time I Saw Paris." Her voice is used
contrapuntally with film of the Nazi takeover of Paris and will be discussed in greater detail later in the chapter.

Music in the "Why We Fight" series is abundant. It is perhaps
over-used. There are very few sequences which do not contain some
form of music. In Prelude to War, music is heard in forty-eight of
of the total fifty minutes. Music fills fifty-eight of the sixty-
three minutes in War Comes to America and seventy-six out of eighty
in The Battle of Russia. The same pattern holds true for all the films

except <u>Divide and Conquer;</u> primarily because of its training film
nature, including the long sequence involving Colonel Clear, music
occupies only forty of its fifty-two minutes. James Agee,in a review
of <u>Prelude to War,</u> states, "Over-all the film is so crowded and so
ramified that it has no ultimate musical coherence."[10] There are
abrupt switches in music necessitated by the literal association of
the music to the visuals. This at times seems jarring. When the
visuals change or the narration switches, the music follows suit. It
rarely carries over or supplies transitions. The films are generally
fast-paced. Thus, the viewer is often bombarded with a succession of
visual images designed to make a complete whole. When the music
attempts to follow this pace, the result is sometimes chaotic. In <u>The</u>
<u>Nazis Strike,</u> for example, Britain and France are mentioned in the same
sentence. Underneath France is "The Marseilles" and then an abrupt cut
is made to the British national anthem when Britain is mentioned. Thus,
rather than unifying, the music oftens bombards the senses and at times
creates a lack of coherence.

Characteristics

The music has three basic characteristics. It is elementary,
repetitive and has immediate appeal.

Elementary

First of all, there is little that is complicated about the music.
Simplicity is a key theme. This can best be seen in the great use of
well-known tunes to characterize scenes and denote place. Whenever
France is mentioned, "The Marseilles" is heard. Whenever Britain is

mentioned we hear the British national anthem. The same is true of
Germany, Italy and Japan. Although the music behind these three
countries is unfamiliar, it is simple and is used continuously with
reference to a particular country. The various religious sequences in
the films utilize well-known hymns, both sung and played, including
"It Came Upon a Midnight Clear" and "Onward Christian Soldier," among
others. In War Comes to America, "Rhapsody in Blue" is used over
visuals describing the growth and power of America's material wealth.
In The Battle of Russia, "The Nutcracker Suite" accompanies a Christmas
scene. In The Nazis Strike, "The Polonaise" is heard under the siege
of Warsaw. In War Comes to America and Prelude to War, "My Country 'Tis
of Thee" is used as a basic characterizing theme for the United States.
"This is the Army, Mr. Jones" is used in War Comes to America over the
sequence depicting the first peace time draft.

Repetitious

Another characteristic of the music is that it is repetitious.
The same basic theme is heard whenever reference is made to Germany.
It is an ominous, dark "invented" theme reflecting the general atmosphere of the Nazi movement. The same general oriental music is heard
with reference to Japan. This pattern holds true for all the films.
Repetition is also employed with somber music played over shots of
bodies and people weeping. The sound attempts to conjure up the
association with past images of Axis cruelty and tie together the
victims of Nazi, Italian and Japanese aggression.

Immediate Appeal

A third characteristic of the music is its immediate appeal.
This appeal is at least partly based on the use of well-known tunes.
The image conjured up is immediate, requiring little or no thought.
In scenes involving religion, "religious" music is always played,
even if it does not consist of well-known hymns. In scenes showing
the general suffering by the civilian population, the somber music
has an immediate appeal. Whenever fighting scenes are accompanied by
music, the music is stirring and action-oriented. The music in this
respect is closely tied to the visuals and/or the narration. To say
the music is appropriate to the visuals is a distinct understatement.
The music is almost literal in its interpretation of the visuals.
When the visuals are fast, showing movement or conveying action, the
music is fast and action-oriented. When the visuals move slowly,
utilizing pans and dissolves, the music underneath is slow and somber.
Thus, the music is usually appropriate to the scene and aids in the
understanding of the theme. Where the visuals alone might confuse,
the music unifies and aids to clarify the scene.

Functions

Atmosphere

The music in the "Why We Fight" films is basically atmospheric.
It tends to unify a number of shots rather than highlight or point to
specific detail. The music attempts to reflect the essential atmosphere of the visuals. When Japan is referred to, the music is definitely
oriental. Ominous theme music is used when Germany is described. Religious scenes utilize definite religious music, slow and somber. In

Prelude to War, during the mobilization of Ethiopia, the music emphasizes the native excitement in the sequence. The Axis powers' music is always heavily drum-cadenced suggesting an overpowering and threatening atmosphere. In War Comes to America, when Japan invades Manchuria, the music is dramatic and full of excitement, again reflecting the general atmosphere of the scene. Thus, the music provides atmosphere and complements scenes, especially scenes of action.

Music often will anticipate action, as in The Battle of Britain when it reflects in ominous, building tones the flight of the Luftwaffe over the Channel. As Roger Manvell has stated, "The inter-relationship of music and action is the commonest form of film music, along with music establishing mood."[11] The "Why We Fight" series makes abundant use of this function. In reflecting specific places or countries, the music is very literal. Tiomkin stated that he often utilized the folk-tunes of a particular country to characterize it. This is especially true in The Battle of Russia where a chorus sings a variety of Russian folk songs.

Emotion

A second major function of the music is to add to or establish the emotional quality of a scene. Its greatest impact seems to be in this area. Tiomkin, in a personal interview, stated that he composed for emotion. He stated that while composing he often became so overwhelmed and caught up in the nature of the film that he literally cried.[12]

The emotions suggested or amplified by the music are varied. In Prelude to War, for example, intense fast telegraphic-like music helps to build dramatic tension in a scene describing the incessant flow of

propaganda coming from Germany. In War Comes to America, America's
growth in material wealth and power is accompanied by "Rhapsody in
Blue." Its driving, intense rhythm heightens the power of the sequence.
Also in War Comes to America, a chorus sings "My Country 'Tis of Thee"
over an animation showing states appearing on a map of the United
States. The appearance of the states is cut to the rhythm of the music
and the entire sequence imparts the power and relentless nature of the
growth of the United States into a complete nation. In The Battle of
China, the narrator states: ". . . and now the call to arms sounded";
the music cuts in with a bugle call. As the visuals show the gradual
building up of a powerful army, the bugle call becomes incorporated
into a bigger and bigger theme symbolizing and emphasizing China's
awakening.

The music also imparts a light, airy mood as well. In Prelude
to War, when the visuals show American children at play, the music is
light and happy, reflecting the mood of the children. This is contrasted with dark, somber, ominous music underneath shots of German,
Italian and Japanese children marching and drilling. Some music portrays a heroic mood and amplifies the emotion of pride. This was especially apparent in The Battle of Russia. The surge of the Russian
army driving the Germans from Russian towns is greatly intensified by
a chorus singing the Russian national anthem. In The Nazis Strike, the
heroic fight of the people of Warsaw to save their city is greatly
amplified by "The Polonaise" playing under the entire sequence. In
The Battle of China, somber march music adds to the heroic nature of
the Chinese trek westward. There are no drums in this particular

march, as drums were used to symbolize the Axis powers. Instead, the
beat of the march is carried by strings. Here, too, the music builds
and grows as the march grows culminating in a chorus singing of the
strength of the people.

Most of the music used for emotion was to intensify the feeling
of grief and sorrow for the civilian populations hurt by the war. The
common man was a distinct theme in the films, both as a positive fighting force against the Axis powers and as the innocent victim of enemy
cruelty. It was this theme of the suffering of the common man that
the music most often and best intensified. In The Nazis Strike, shots
of dead bodies and people weeping are amplified by the suffering
quality of the music. The pace in this sequence is slow and the music
fits the pace. The same music underlies shots of refugees on the roads
of France in Divide and Conquer. The music adds the element of pathos
which is not inherent in the shots themselves. Pathos reflected in
music is very apparent in The Battle of China, where the music contributes to the sense of suffering of the civilian population of Nanking.
The music in most of these cases is not recognizable but somber and
classical in nature. In The Battle of Russia, music also intensifies
shots of dead children and ravaged girls. However, here the music not
only emphasizes the suffering inherent in the shots, but adds a note
of heroic grief and a determination to see it through. In The Battle
of Britain, shots of the people of Coventry burying their dead is
accompanied by "Auld Lang Syne." The combination of the familiar
music with its happy-sad associations and the shots of people weeping
over loved ones creates a powerful emotional impact.

There are few instances of contrapuntal sound in the "Why We
Fight" series. However, one instance in particular provided perhaps
the most dramatic impact of the entire series. The scene occurs in
War Comes to America. An American family is shown listening to the
radio as William L. Shirer describes the French surrender. The visual
cuts to the scene Shirer is describing, then cuts back to the family
listening as Shirer concludes, "The whole ceremony is over in less
than an hour." The father becomes disgusted and switches channels.
A woman's voice sings "The Last Time I Saw Paris." The visuals then
cut to shots of German-occupied Paris. The song describes full cafes,
busy streets and laughing people. The visuals, however, show empty
streets, empty cafes, people weeping, German troops marching through
the streets and a Nazi laughing in the face of the camera. A strong
impact is intended. Another example of contrapuntal sound is in The
Battle of Russia. It is much less forceful and dramatic than the first
example. The visuals show a road bed being plowed across a lake. The
shots are quite pedestrian, showing men plowing. However, the music
is heroic adding meaning to the scene not inherent in the shots and
somewhat against the grain of the shot meaning itself. A final example
occurs in Prelude to War. In a sequence depicting the abolishment of
religion in Germany, the hymn, "O Come All Ye Faithful," is heard over
scenes of churches being closed and newspapers headlining the imprison-
ment of pastors and closing of churches.

Outside of music used for atmosphere and for emotion, the rest
of the music is used essentially as background. The narration almost
always has this "nondescript" music underneath it. The long instructional and descriptive passages also have background music. The music

fills out the void in scenes which might be barren without it. The
music is somewhat similar in both style and function to that played
in department stores over intercom systems. It envelopes the listener
in a warm bath of music, fills out the empty spaces and soon becomes so
familiar and common it lapses into a state of not being heard at all.
This is not to be taken as a negative comment. It is often this function of not standing out that makes it effective.

SUMMARY

In summary, the sound track of the "Why We Fight" series is
appropriate. When one considers the audience for which the series--
hence the sound--was meant (thirty-seven percent of the troops not
having gone to high school) and the speed with which the series had to
be made, it is clearly understandable why the sound tracks exhibit the
characteristics they do.

It is true, when viewed by modern standards and when the nature
of the audience the films were created for is disregarded, the sound
seems overwhelming and at times superfluous. However, these films
were designed to inform and convince a large body of men, some of them
illiterate, about the reasons they were fighting. The messages of the
films needed to be clear, concise and to the point. The sound track
aided the accomplishment of these goals.

Speech, particularly the narration, dominated the sound track.
It functioned to instruct, impress and to create variety. It also
built up the tension and excitement of passages and often punctuated
the film. For the most part, the speech blended in well with the total
film. There were a few instances where the narration perhaps called

attention to itself by being overdramatic, but in general it did not stand out. Its basic function was to aid understanding. It did this without sounding like a lecture or becoming boring.

Natural sounds were used "plastically" in the films. They were not used to merely duplicate the visuals, but rather helped to establish the reality and atmosphere of a scene. They were especially useful in creating an image of war. At times they were the only sound track element utilized, and still the impact and reality of a scene was not lost. They, too, blended in with the rest of the elements of film structure. There were even several instances where they conveyed the emotion of a scene (Japanese, German and Italian crowds yelling).

The music in the films was simple. It essentially functioned to create atmosphere, to unify scenes and to aid understanding. The music, more than any other element of the sound track, provided emotion. As Tiomkin stated, he composed for emotion. Whether it was a well-known popular tune, a hymn or "invented" music, the music functioned to convey emotion. Its appeal was immediate. If the visuals or narrator did not adequately communicate to the audience the emotion or information in a scene, the music often did. At time, the abrupt switches in music to coincide with the rapid pace of the switches in visuals perhaps created some chaos and may have seemed "jerky," but the music rarely confused the audience.

Thus, in essence, the sound track functioned in a variety of ways with a variety of means to perform two basic functions: to aid and/or create understanding, and to aid and/or create emotion. Sound was used extensively in all the films. However, rarely did it stand out and call attention to itself. It blended in with the visual structure of the films to create a total film statement. It was more than sound used to duplicate the visuals; it was sound used "plastically" to interpret, inform and convince.

FOOTNOTES - CHAPTER V

[1]Burton Stevenson (ed.), The Home Book of Quotations (New York: Dodd, Mead & Company, 1967), p. 602.

[2]Arthur Knight, The Liveliest Art (New York: Mentor, 1957), p. 143.

[3]Karel Reisz, The Techniques of Film Editing (New York: Focal Press, Ltd., 1958), p. 197.

[4]Hugh Baddeley, The Technique of Documentary Film Production (New York: Focal Press, Ltd., 1963), p. 191.

[5]James Agee, Agee on Film (New York: McDowell Obolensky, Inc., 1958), p. 40.

[6]Ibid., p. 66.

[7]Baddeley, p. 193.

[8]C. I. Hovland, A. A. Lumsdaine, and F. D. Sheffield, Experiments on Mass Communication (New York: John Wiley & Sons, Inc., 1965), p. 22.

[9]Roger Manvell, The Technique of Film Music (New York: Focal Press, Ltd., 1957), p. 59.

[10]Agee, p. 40.

[11]Manvell, p. 74.

[12]Dimitri Tiomkin, private interview, October 19, 1967.

CHAPTER VI

VISUAL STYLE

INTRODUCTION

This chapter is a description and analysis of the visual elements
of the "Why We Fight" series. Despite the major contribution sound
makes to the films, it is the visual structure which provides much of
the impact and distinctive quality of the films. This structure consists of a number of elements. Each of them contributes to the films
in different ways and with varying degrees of importance.

There are two major areas of consideration in the visual structure
of a film. The first area is the shot itself and the elements which are
contained within this unit. This is what Reynolds terms "intra-shot"
considerations. Here, the analyst is concerned with camera angle,
camera movement, lens angle, lighting, acting, setting, and special
optical effects such as superimpositions. The second area is what
Reynolds terms "inter-shot" techniques.[1] The concern here is with the
standard transitions (the cut, the fade, the dissolve, the wipe) and
shot length. From these "inter-shot" elements evolve patterns of
editing.

Definitions

Editing

The primary method of altering the view on the screen is by
editing. This change is effected by filming different views of a

subject, selecting the shots desired and assembling them in coherent sequences, which, when projected, form the scenes, sequences and episodes of a complete film. The stress is upon assembly, the total effect of shots in combination with one another.

Montage

The term has several meanings. It was used by early Russian directors as a synonym for creative editing. In France it is still used to denote cutting. However, in British and American studios, it usually means a quick impressionistic sequence of disconnected images, usually linked by dissolves, superimpositions, or wipes, and used to convey passages of time, changes of place, or any other types of transition. Montage is also used to effect changes in meaning and other "subjective" uses. One of the most famous examples of this is in Orson Welle's Citizen Kane, where the deterioration of the marriage is shown through a montage of the couple eating breakfast over a period of time.

Transitions

Within editing, the method of changing from one shot to another may be accomplished in a variety of ways. Thus, transitions become important. Shot-change may be effected by a cut (one image replaces another instantly), fade-out or fade-in (one image fades into black and the next image comes in from black), dissolve (as the old image disappears, the new one appears resulting in the two being superimposed for a short time), wipe (a line passes across the screen wiping out the old image and replacing it with a new one), and iris (the old image fades from the edges of the screen to the center and the new image emerges in a widening circle from the center of the screen). These constitute the basic means of effecting shot-change.

Length of Shot

Another element to be considered in relation to the editing pattern is the length of the shot. Such frame counting aids in establishing the basic rhythm and cutting speed of the film. It provides only a basic outline of the editing pattern, however.

Camera Movement

The other basic means of altering the picture on the screen is by camera movement, of which there are several types. When the entire camera moves, it is called trucking. If the camera is kept stationary but moved on its axis laterally, this is known as panning. A similar movement vertically is called tilting.

Lens Angle

The extent of the view on the screen and its scale depends on the distance of the camera from the objects photographed and the lens used. There are an infinite number of possibilities, but generally the distance of the subject from the camera is characterized by seven terms: (1) extreme close up, (2) close up, (3) medium close up, (4) medium shot, (5) medium long shot, (6) long shot, (7) extreme long shot.

Camera Angle

Camera angle refers to the angle of view with which the camera photographs a particular object or event. This position of the camera is referred to as a shooting angle. Again, there are an infinite number of possible angles ranging from vertically downward through horizontal to vertically upward.

Optical Variations

There are several visual effects which do not fall under any of the previous categories. Such elements as superimpositions, split screens, out-of-focus shots, stop motion, slow motion, among others, create certain specific effects in a film. They are for the most part created in a film laboratory, and in many instances, add to a film's effectiveness.

Content

All of the aforementioned elements contribute to film communication. They are all tools by which content is conveyed. Thus, the subject matter and its characteristics also perform a key role in the communication of a film's message.

Within the shot there are several elements of content which are important. Among them are acting, lighting and setting. In the "Why We Fight" series these elements have less importance than in entertainment film. Elements of content which are especially important in the "Why We Fight" films are titles and animations.

There are, to be sure, other technical elements regarding the visual elements of film. However, such theorists and critics as Arnheim, Spottiswoode, Kracauer and others confirm that those previsouly reviewed, along with sound, constitute the basic elements of the film medium.

The Compilation Film

Because the "Why We Fight" films are all compilation films, some
of the elements previously mentioned take on greater significance than
others. The compilation form is composed, for the most part, of newsreel and similar material which has not been scripted or shot for the
purpose of the particular film in which it is being used. Thus, the
director of the compilation film is generally without the advantages
of a planned shooting script, directed performance from actors, control
over lighting, sets, camera angle, lens angle and properly interrelating shots. The compilation director's basic assets are his skill
as an editor and his ability to illustrate and exploit the suggestive
power of the narration. Thus, while most of the basic elements of the
visual structure of the "Why We Fight" films will be discussed, their
use and importance to a certain extent are determined by the form of
the films themselves.

ELEMENTS OF VISUAL STRUCTURE

Eight basic visual elements were isolated and analyzed in the
"Why We Fight" series. They are: (1) camera angle, (2) lens angle,
(3) camera movement, (4) content, (5) optical variations, (6) transitions, (7) length of shot, and (8) editing. These elements are not
arbitrary with the researcher. Virtually every film theorist and
critic regards them as basic to the nature of film.

Each of the visual elements in the films will be analyzed in two
ways: (1) characteristics, and (2) function. Implications of each of
these elements are established, using as criteria the universally

accepted theories of such critics and theorists as Spottiswoode,

Arnheim and Kracauer, as well as personal observation.

Intra-Shot Elements

Camera Angle

As Rudolf Arnheim stated,

> Thus, the conditions under which the picture is
> taken (in our example the choice of a particular
> angle of approach) are not treated as negligible
> quantities or necessary evils, but are consciously
> brought into relief as factors contributing to
> composition of the picture.[2]

Camera angle in the "Why We Fight" series was an element in which the

makers of the films had choice but not control. The fact that almost

all of the footage with the exception of a few studio scenes was not

shot specifically for the films in the series limited the subjective

and artistic use of camera angle.

Characteristics. Every shot in the films has a particular camera

angle. Thus, any quantitative breakdown is meaningless. However, the

extent to which camera angle was used to perform certain functions can

be analyzed.

Function. Camera angles perform several distinct functions in a

film. They convey content, characterize an object or person, satisfy

the requirements of pure form, force the spectator to take keener

interest, interpret or suggest and add variety by splitting up a scene.

Camera angle performs all of these functions in the "Why We Fight"

films.

Convey action or shot content.--This represents the greatest use

of camera angle in the films--not surprising in that the bulk of the footage is newsreel, particularly war action footage. The obvious purpose in this footage is to convey the action and content of the scene photographed. With much of it being actual combat footage, the photographer's concern with camera angle is obviously not so much with providing a psychological effect or splitting up a scene to add variety, as getting the action of the scene without getting killed. There are, in a number of instances, particularly in Divide and Conquer, very poor (they convey little content; the camera appears to shake; the view may be blocked) shots in terms of camera angle, but they were included because they were the only material available.

Characterization of an object or person.--There was little use of this function in the films. Again, the footage and circumstances under which most of it was shot precluded, for the most part, the use of camera angle consciously to characterize an object or person. There are, however, some examples which should be mentioned. In Prelude to War, Nazi stormtroopers are characterized as stern, powerful figures by shooting down a line of them from an upward angle toward their faces. The lantern jaws and harsh helmets effectively characterize these men.

It should be noted that this film was shot by German cameramen. The intent of the angle originally was most likely to portray the German soldier as a superhuman creature, an individual bigger than life. This footage was taken by Capra and "twisted" to portray an alternate meaning; here the footage was used to portray the German soldier as an object of fear. This particular "twisting" of footage is not uncommon in the "Why We Fight" films. In Divide and Conquer,

film of French refugees being strafed by Nazi divebombers was used in
a German film to portray the swift and all powerful nature of the Nazi
Blitzkrieg; in Divide and Conquer, the film is used to depict "A new low
in Nazi brutality." This "twisting" points up the adaptability of the
compilation form. It also points out the need for the careful editing
and placement of shots and the close tie-up with the narration.

In The Battle of Britain, several instances of this use of camera
angle occur. In shots 397-404 the narrator states that the German
bombers are protected by fighters above, below, to the front, rear and
weaving in and out of the formations. As each of the angles is mentioned, an appropriately angled shot of German fighters is shown.
Fighters to the rear is a front shot; fighters in front is a rear angle
shot; fighters below is an above shot, and so on. Camera angle is
used in The Battle of Britain to characterize several objects which
might prove confusing if not unidentifiable. Several shots of listening posts with radar cones taken from a low angle looking up identify
the objects as sky-oriented. This angle, coupled with the narration,
establishes the nature of the object.

Perhaps the most consistent use of camera angle to characterize
is in the use of low, "shooting-up" angles when showing churches, presenting low angle shots of church steeples and stained glass windows.
This aids in the characterization of the churches as lofty, inspiring
forces in society. There were also several instances of crowd shots
taken from an overhead angle. This particular angle, especially in
reference to the huge crowds listening to Hitler speak, effectively
characterizes the crowd as a teeming mass, not as individuals. Here,

again, the footage is "twisted". Outside of these instances, however, little use is made of this function.

Satisfy requirements of pure form.--This camera angle function supplies no meaning in the film. Its use is characterized by an angled or tilted shot inserted for pure form, perhaps to add variety. The greatest use of this function is in War Comes to America. Several times tilted angles of common objects are used. There seems to be no meaning or symbolic comment involved. In the sequence describing the inventiveness of the American people (246-260), tilted shots of a tele- graph key, a gyroscope and a woman sewing are cut in with shots utilizing a realistic angle. This function is also used in the sequences depicting the various nationalities that make up the people of the United States. There is no reason for the particular angle other than pure form and to produce variety in the sequence. The use is also found in Prelude to War and The Nazis Strike, where above, oblique angles are used to show German troops marching. If these angles were emphasized consistently and more shots were used, the use might fall under the Eisenstein "montage of angles" category. However, usually only one shot is used. Thus, it functions as pure form to introduce variety.

Force spectator to take keener interest.--This is found very in- frequently in the films. This function is usually supplied by the narrator and lens angle, and in some cases, editing. However, a few instances of this camera angle function do exist. In The Nazis Strike, a low angle shot of a lit star introducing a sequence describing Russian preparation for war concentrates viewer attention. In Divide and Conquer, a low front angle shot of several people on bikes riding into the camera forces spectator attention to the fact that the Nazis utilized every means of transportation in their Blitzkrieg.

Interpretation and symbolic comment.--This function is not used frequently. The films are basically realistic and informative in terms of their visual structure and thus there is little use for symbolic camera angles that might confuse the viewer. Also, of course, the fact of choice and non-control over camera angle hinders this particular use of it. Most of the suggestion and interpretation, when there is any, is left to the narration and in some cases the music. However, there are several instances where this function does exist. In all of the films, ground level shots of German troops marching, emphasizing their legs and boots, suggests the overpowering nature of the German attack. This effect is also achieved in Divide and Conquer,where low-angle shots of tank treads produces the same overpowering effect.

A shot somewhat dissimilar to the previous ones occurs in Prelude to War. Here, a ground level shot of the bare feet of the Ethiopian army illustrates their lack of power. This shot juxtaposed against a series of shots emphasizing Italy's strength, strongly suggests the comparative strength of the two countries and is intended to make Italy look a little foolish.

In camera angle, then, it is the content and basic form of the films that dominates the sense of camera angle. The films are essentially designed to portray realistically the causes and events leading up to the war. The compilation form is utilized to convey this information. Thus, the basic function of camera angle is to convey content and action in a particular shot. Here also, the fact that

there is choice but not control of camera angle limits its functions.
Thus, the necessity to portray events realistically dominates the use
of camera angle. The few instances of conscious concern for camera
angle in a subjective sense occur in studio production shots and in
the scenes taken from commercial motion picture features.

Lens Angle

Here also, as with camera angle, because much of the footage is
combat footage, and was shot to convey content and action and not for
symbolic effect, realism dominates the use of lens angle.

Use. Because much of the footage is newsreel and combat footage
and was in all likelihood shot with a hand-held camera dictates some
use of camera angle. Combat photography for the most part is unable
to produce close ups and extreme close ups. Thus, long shots, medium
long shots and medium shots predominate in the films, although the use
of close ups is by no means insignificant. The following table lists
the percentage of shots of the named types. Such a table must necessarily only suggest the lens angle since the cataloging of each shot
involved a personal judgment.

TABLE I

	ECU	CU	MCU	MS	MLS	LS	ELS
Prelude to War	4%	13%	8%	20%	18%	30%	7%
The Nazis Strike	3%	4%	7%.	24%	18%	37%	7%
Divide and Conquer	2%	11%	9%	20%	23%	25%	10%
The Battle of Britain	2%	7%	9%	22%	20%	31%	9%
The Battle of Russia	3%	12%	9%	20%	17%	32%	7%
War Comes to America	3%	11%	9%	18%	19%	30%	10%
Average	3%	9.6%	9%	20%	19%	31%	8%

ie greater percentage of medium shots, medium long shots and long

iots points up the combat and general "action" orientation of most of

ie footage. Most of the scenes were shot with a hand-held camera from

ie set-up. There was little opportunity to get close ups of the action.

lso, to portray an event or scene with CU's takes a great amount of

elated footage. This is something the makers of the "Why We Fight"

ilms did not have.

This data, as well as that tabulated for the other film elements,

annot be compared with similar data for other films. The four previous

tudies (two by Huff, one each by Kuiper and Byrne) utilizing shot analy-

is were all conducted with silent, commercial, studio-made motion

ictures. This makes any comparison of figures illogical.

Function. Lens angle in the "Why We Fight" series performed four

asic functions: (1) emphasize an object to gain audience attention,

!) convey meaning and introduce detail, (3) interpretation and sym-

olic comment, and (4) split up a sequence--variety.

Emphasis of a particular object to gain audience attention.--This

inction is used in all the films with some frequency. The shot types

ost commonly employed for this function are the ECU and CU. In The

attle of Britain,in a sequence involving RAF pilots getting out of

ieir planes after a German attack, an ECU of a bullet hole in a plane

3 cut in to show the fury of the battle. Also in The Battle of Britain,

CU of a map of London is cut in when the narrator poses the rhetorical

iestion of where the Nazis would strike next. The audience's atten-

ion is first gained visually by the CU; then the battle for London

egins. In The Nazis Strike, a CU of a bruised arm draws audience attention to Nazi brutality in Belgium. Another example in this film is a CU of Hitler following shots of a map with the narrator describing the Nazi plan for world conquest. Here the viewer is seemingly jolted from a relatively passive scene to an active one. In Prelude to War, a CU of a drumhead being beaten follows a LS of Japanese children and draws audience attention to a German youth parade. In Divide and Conquer, the first shot following the opening titles is a CU of a man wearing a body sign with "WAR" in large letters on it. In the same film, a "live" CU of General Foch following several long shots of statues gains audience attention. In War Comes to America, an ECU of the Liberty Bell following several medium long shots of paintings draws audience attention.

Convey meaning and introduce detail.--This function is effected most frequently by varied utilization of lens angle in the films. Throughout the films, medium close ups and close ups are intercut into scenes to convey meaning and introduce detail. In War Comes to America, CU's of the clock in the State Department showing the passage of time on December 7, 1941, convey meaning. In The Battle of Britain, a CU of a British pilot giving the thumbs up sign after shooting down a German fighter also conveys meaning. In Prelude to War, a CU of gleaming belt buckles following an MLS of German troops adds detail to a sequence of marching German troops. In Divide and Conquer, a CU of a newsheet with "A Call to Arms" printed on it conveys in a single shot the meaning of the French mobilization. In The Nazis Strike, an MS of a radio tower conveys the meaning that the "Polonaise" is being played on the radio during the siege of Warsaw.

Meaning is also conveyed by long shots and extreme long shots. In several instances, aerial shots of burning cities convey the totality of destruction much more than could a series of close shots. In The Battle of Britain, an aerial shot of fires burning all over London communicates the extent of the fire. In The Nazis Strike and War Comes to America, ELS's of the Nazi rally at Nuremberg reveal the Nazis' use of mass behavior and pageantry. In Prelude to War, an ELS of Japanese planes flying over the tops of buildings in Shanghai conveys the meaning of the overpowering nature of the Japanese air attack.

Interpretation and symbolic comment.--This is the least employed function of lens angle in the films. Very few individual shots, and thus lens angles, carry symbolic meaning by themselves. However, a few instances do appear. In Prelude to War, a CU of an old bearded man with a somewhat dazed expression on his face follows a long sequence showing the might of the German army marching through Berlin. The shot is held for over five seconds and then slowly dissolves into a shot of a dark globe. Here, the shot is a symbolic comment on the reaction of some of the German people to the rise of the Nazi Party. Throughout the films, but particularly in The Nazis Strike, CU's of tank treads are used to suggest the Nazi blitz. The effect of an unstoppable machine rolling over a country is conveyed. In The Battle of Britain, a CU of a uniformed man with a rifle over one shoulder picking up a bottle of milk and the morning paper on his front stoop is symbolic of the concept of the British people fighting the war as a home guard. In War Comes to America, ECU's of German boots marching across the screen are symbolic of the German attack. The tank treads and boots are often used to describe the fall of a particular country to the

Germans. This CU is a symbol that the attack has begun.

Spit up a sequence--variety.--This function receives emphasis

in the films second in extent only to that of conveying meaning. This

function is continually found in short montage sequences depicting a

concept or a particular action. The greatest use of this function is

found in Divide and Conquer and The Battle of Britain. Divide and

Conquer is essentially an "action"picture, describing the fall of the

Low Countries. Thus, the attack on each country is presented almost

exclusively in chronological organization. These battle sequences are

then split up by the use of different shots and different lens angles

to provide variety. In The Battle of Britain, this function is exten-

sively used in dog fight sequences. The following shot sequence reflects

this use:

314. LS German plane
315. CU German pilot
316. MCU Two German pilots in same plane
317. MLS British plane
318. CU German pilot
319. CU Hand moving to stick
320. MS Underside of German plane
321. LS German plane with British plane following.
322. LS British plane diving and firing
323. LS German plane followed by British plane
324. MLS Plane wheeling to right
325. CU German pilot being shot
326. LS German plane smoking
327. ELS Smoking German plane diving into ground.

This sequence might have been shot with all long shots and extreme

long shots; the intercutting of CU's added variety to the sequence.

Examples of all these lens angle functions are found in all the

films. Those cited, in most instances, are merely illustrative of the

way the function is found in the films. Lens angle performs a more flexible role than camera angle in the "Why We Fight" films. This is partly because lens angle can and does provide a variety of realistic functions. Thus, it is used with greater flexibility and plays a greater role in the communication of the message than camera angle.

Camera Movement

Use. The following table indicates the percentage of shots in each film which contain camera movement.

TABLE II

Prelude to War	9%
The Nazis Strike	13%
Divide and Conquer	9%
The Battle of Britain	10%
The Battle of Russia	5%
War Comes to America	7%

It can be seen from this table that two of the action-oriented films, The Nazis Strike and The Battle of Britain, contain the most camera movement. The movement in the combat footage, which makes up a great deal of the films' sequences, is necessary in order to follow the action.

Function. Camera movement in the films provides for a variety of functions. They are for the most part realistically motivated.

Follow action.--This is by far the greatest function of camera movement in the films. The films are basically action-oriented, some more than others. Thus, there is a great deal of camera movement for the purpose of following the action. This is especially true, as has been noted, in The Nazis Strike and The Battle of Britain. In The

Battle of Britain much of the footage is of air action and thus camera
movement is almost a requisite. All through the films the camera is a
mobile instrument revealing action to the audience.

Presentation of details and reaction.--This is also a great function of camera movement. It often occurs as the narrator refers to a
particular detail or piece of action. Slow pans across rubble and
wreckage reveal the extent of damage. In Prelude to War, a long trucking shot reveals the great damage done at Pearl Harbor, In The Nazis
Strike, slow pans across stacks of tires and bales of wire reveal the
extent of the United States' aid to England. In The Battle of Britain,
a trucking shot forward over two men's shoulders to a huge map reveals
an airplane plotting board. In War Comes to America, the camera tilts
down slowly over the Declaration of Independence to the signatures at
the bottom. In Divide and Conquer, the camera pans slowly over an
audience listening to Hitler speak, revealing the intensity with which
they are listening. In Prelude to War, the camera zooms in on a
portrait of Hitler as it is revealed through a broken stained glass
window. In The Nazis Strike, the camera pans from German soldiers
carrying banners up a flight of stairs to a shot of Hitler standing
over them on a stone platform. Another example of this function occurs
in The Battle of Britain. The camera focuses on a sedate English house
and then slowly pans to reveal a British bomber hidden under trees in
the front yard. The emphasis here is upon the courage and intelligence
of the British people in not placing their planes on the airfields. In
War Comes to America, the camera focuses on a mother holding her child
and then slowly pans to reveal the mother trying to warm her hands and
the child's feet over a small fire.

Characterize objects or locales.--This function is found infrequently in the films, but there are instances where it is utilized to good advantage. In Prelude to War, the camera focuses on a studio shot of a German general being shot and then tilts up to a picture on the wall of Von Hindenberg being riddled with bullets. This tilt characterizes the General as old line and loyal to the old order and thus the reason for his extermination is communicated. In The Nazis Strike, the camera slowly pans and tilts down from a line of soldiers on a hill to hundreds of people working. This shot shows the use of forced labor in Germany. Another instance of this function occurs in The Battle of Britain. The camera focuses down on the rear of three German soldiers in a bunker and then tilts up to reveal the North Sea in front of them. This visually characterizes the Germans being on the coast of France and looking to England. In War Comes to America, several trucking shots through the streets of Paris dramatically characterize the locale. The sound on the film is a voice singing "The Last Time I Saw Paris," with specific reference at this point to gay and people-filled streets. The camera moving along deserted streets offers an effective contrast and heightens the dramatic sense of the passage.

This, then, characterizes the use and function of camera movement in the "Why We Fight" films. Again, as in camera and lens angle, the basic function of this cinematic tool is to present scenes, places and people realistically. The emphasis is to present visual information clearly and to aid understanding.

Content

The subject matter of the films was for the most part "live" action. Much of the material was combat footage, while other unstaged footage was gathered from newsreels and documentaries. Typical of the films is The Battle of Russia. The total footage of this film was 7,363 feet, which was considerably longer than the other films. However, the source percentage of the material making up this footage was typical of the other films. Of this total amount, 4,542 feet was Russian film from various feature productions, documentary films and newsreels. Enemy-seized film made up 496 feet. There was 77 feet from various allied documentary films and 500 feet from American newsreel and studio-made material.[3]

In terms of live content there is little to comment on. Here, again, the content was a matter of choice rather than control. Thus, elements such as acting, lighting and decor were not consciously controlled in the films. There are several instances where voices are dubbed in, but the attempts are obvious, and according to the troops' own reaction, "ineffective."[4] In The Battle of Russia, for example, a shot of a yelling Russian officer includes an obviously dubbed command. The same is true in The Battle of Britain, where a CU of a German pilot shouting "Spitfire" is shown.

Lighting. Lighting in the films is not a conscious element of production. The only light present in most of the footage is that which was naturally there. In the night shots of London being bombed, it is difficult at times to make out the figures, the only illumination being gun flashes and fires. This did, however, add to the realism of the shots.

Setting. Setting and decor were, like lighting, not consciously controlled in the films. The settings are "real" in the ultimate sense of the word.

Studio Scenes. There are several studio-produced sequences in all the films, especially in The Battle of Russia and The Battle of Britain. These studio scenes are fairly obvious in their "faked" reality and were the subject of frequent criticism by the troops.[5] However, in most cases they provide variety and supplement live footage which was not available for certain scenes. In The Battle of Britain, small vignettes of people in the blitz provide a break in the stream of footage depicting planes, bombs and ruined buildings. The same is true of several scenes in The Battle of Russia, although, here, several "faked" ambush scenes are almost comical in contrast to the real horror of war displayed in combat footage. For the most part, however, the studio shots are used discriminatingly and blend in well with the live footage. In War Comes to America, studio shots of Japanese planes attacking air fields at Pearl Harbor, American soldiers firing back and wounded men lying on the ground are realistic. In this instance, and many others, the only way the studio footage can be identified as such is by the "glossy" quality of the film, the subjective use of camera angles, and, in some instances, the presence of dialogue. For the most part, the acting is low key and realistic and the setting and lighting are natural. The one obvious deviation from this occurs in The Battle of Russia where a long panning shot down the faces of Russian guerrillas reciting an oath is obviously lit for dramatic effect.

The only other aspect of acting in the films is the use of voices with heavy German, Italian and Japanese accents. This technique is employed once in The Nazis Strike and three times in War Comes to America. The emphasis here is to stereotype the various Axis powers and make the appeal of the accent immediately recognizable.

Titles and Animation. The other two elements of content in the films are titles and animations.

Use.--These two elements are used frequently in all the films. The following table indicates the number of shots which contain titles or are composed of animations.

TABLE III

	Shots Which Contain Titles	Shots Which Contain Animations
Prelude to War	54	56
The Nazis Strike	31	36
Divide and Conquer	26	38
The Battle of Britain	26	21
The Battle of Russia	75	61
War Comes to America	92	61
Average	50	45

This table gives some indication of the filmmakers' concern for clearness of presentation and variety in form. Titles were used frequently in the films, despite the fact that they were sound films. Byrne found that the German expressionistic films averaged 100 titles per film, the lowest number being 38 and the highest 207.[6]

Thus, it can be seen that despite the films being sound, they made heavy use of titles.

Function.--Titles basically function to present factual information to the viewer. In these films they rarely exist alone; the narrator reads them as they are shown on the screen. They consist in each film of the opening title and credits and of Marshall's closing statement. The most extensive use of titles is in giving quotes, especially quotes from Axis leaders, particularly Hitler. Here they are used to present information as clearly as possible. Most of the quote titles are supered over a shot of the scene where the speech is taking place and the individual is delivering it.

Statistics are also put into titles fairly frequently; again the need to present the information as clearly as possible dictates this use of titles. The statistics are again read as they are shown on the screen. This use is especially prevalent in The Battle of Britain, where great emphasis is placed on the odds the RAF faced and on the outcome of the battles with the German fighters and bombers.

There is also extensive use of animation in all the films. These animations were all made at cost by Walt Disney under commercial contract. The animations perform two basic functions in the films. They first function as visual aids; to present information that would otherwise only be talked about. The second function is visual effect. Here the animation communicates no essential information, but does act to produce variety and is intended for emotional effect.

The prime examples of the visual aid animations are those illustrating battle strategy. In Divide and Conquer, animations describe the fall of France and the Low Countries for almost four minutes. Animations clearly illustrate the fall of Poland in The Nazis Strike.

Animations are used in The Battle of Britain to illustrate the Nazis'
three-phase plan for the invasion of England. In The Battle of Russia,
animations are used to illustrate the Russian "defense in depth"
strategy as opposed to the Nazis' "wedge and trap."

Animations are also used to illustrate detailed explanations of
Axis theories and philosophies of world conquest. The concept of geopolitics in The Nazis Strike is depicted by animations which aid clarity
as does the Japanese plan for world conquest as outlined in the Tanaka
Memorial in Prelude to War. Animations in War Comes to America illustrate the United States' position if the Axis powers would succeed in
conquering Europe, Russia and the Far East.

Animations are also used to introduce variety and produce emotion.
In Divide and Conquer, a hand is shown covered with miniature swastikas,
representing spiders. The hand reaches over a wall labeled Belgium and
shakes the swastikas off. One basic form of animation is repeated four
times, once in Prelude to War and The Battle of Russia and twice in War
Comes to America. This is an animation of a huge dagger accompanied by
a bolt of lightning plunging into a country; in these instances, Manchuria three times and the United States once. Another frequent animation form is used to illustrate the Axis takeover of a country or
countries. In one instance, the Nazi swastika drips black-like blood
into Austria and Czechoslovakia. Another time, little swastikas zoom
out of a large one in the middle of Germany and blast like shells into
the Low Countries, turning them black. Another instance in War Comes
to America shows a giant mailed fist stamping France with a swastika.
In all these examples the animation communicates emotional meaning and
introduces visual variety.

Thus, the elements of content in all their various aspects basically function to convey information. Animations and some studio shots provide some interpretation and subjective quality to the films, but essentially the elements of content are designed to facilitate the basic purpose of the films--to inform, to convey information. It is indicative of the prime nature of this informative purpose that a variety of means are used to fulfill it. Rarely is information entrusted to one content element. Rather, a variety of elements, including titles, animations and studio shots, as well as live footage, are used to convey the sense of the message.

Optical Variations

Use. Optical variations in the films take a variety of forms, the most common being the superimposition. Other forms such as split-screen and fast, slow and stop motion are used, but with less frequency. The following table indicates the frequency of optical variations in the films.

TABLE IV

	Super-imposition	Split screen	Fast motion	Slow	Stop
Prelude to War	33	0	0	0	0
The Nazis Strike	37	0	0	0	0
Divide and Conquer	12	0	0	1	1
The Battle of Britain	8	1	0	0	0
The Battle of Russia	36	2	0	0	0
War Comes to America	61	3	37	0	0
Average	31	N.A.	N.A.	N.A.	N.A.

Superimpositions are used in all the films with varying frequency.
Divide and Conquer and The Battle of Britain contain the least because
of their basic action orientation. The great number of fast motion
shots in War Comes to America, are all contained in one sequence. This
is a montage sequence describing the food Americans eat. It is cut
rapidly to fast music and employs all CU's and ECU's. The split screen
effects are employed arbitrarily and seemingly for no other reason than
pure effect. In War Comes to America, one of the split screens has
photographs of Hitler, Mussolini and Hirohito on top of the screen and
a cheering crowd on the bottom. This effect is employed twice. The
other use is a side split screen of workers at a drafting table and a
shot of dynamos on the other side of the screen. In The Battle of
Britain, parachutes are shown on the top of the screen and an animated
drawing of England is on the bottom.

The one instance of stop motion in the films occurs in Divide and
Conquer when the camera freezes and then zooms in on a shot of an American soldier. The individual is the first American soldier to die in
World War II. He was killed in Norway in 1940. The single instance
of slow motion also occurs in Divide and Conquer. The shot is of a
bomb exploding, scattering dirt into the air. There is no apparent
reason for the effect other than to slow the action down to observe
the exploding effect of the bomb. Other than these instances, no
other optical variations are used.

Function. The function of the optical variations are again
basically realistic, although there is more subjective function here
than there is with camera and lens angle.

Superimpositions are employed primarily to indicate relationships between shots, both realistic and symbolic. Perhaps the most striking example of a symbolic relationship occurs in The Nazis Strike. Here, a close up photograph of Hitler is supered over a sequence describing Genghis Khan's conquest of the world. The idea is presented that the two men are alike in their desires for world conquest. A more or less realistic relationship is established by a series of supers in War Comes to America. Here, shots of individual American soldiers marching toward the camera are supered over different locales depicting that the men were from the hills, plains, cities, etc.

Another function of the super is to create the impression of chaos and confusion. This is the customary use of the super in the commercial motion picture. However, it is only used once in the "Why We Fight" films. In Prelude to War, the chaos caused by the postwar inflation in Germany is visualized through several supers of money over bread, coins piling up and price tags being altered.

The only other function of the super was the modification of reality. This occurred in Prelude to War where shots of marching Japanese troops are supered over Pennsylvania Avenue, creating the impression of the troops parading down the streets of Washington.

Thus, optical variations are employed subjectively in the films. However, the extent of their use once again points to the basic informational nature of the films. Any element that hindered the communication of the messages in the films was used infrequently, if at all.

Inter-Shot Elements

Transitions

Use. Transitions in the "Why We Fight" films consist of cuts, fades, dissolves, irises and wipes. The following table gives the percentage of each type for the six films for which shot analysis was possible.

TABLE V

	Cut	Fade	Dissolve	Iris	Wipe
Prelude to War	76%	1%	18%	.1%	4%
Divide and Conquer	95%	.5%	4%	0%	0%
The Nazis Strike	84%	1%	13%	.1%	1%
The Battle of Britain	91%	.3%	5%	.3%	3%
The Battle of Russia	92%	.3%	7%	0%	.7%
War Comes to America	88%	.3%	9%	.8%	2%
Average	88%	.56%	9%	.21%	1.8%

These figures by themselves only suggest the style of the films. The interrelationship of all the elements of film construction provides a truer picture. However, it can be seen that Divide and Conquer and The Battle of Britain were the most "limited" films. They involved little significant change of place or time; whereas Prelude to War involved the interacting of three Axis powers and the United States over a period of twenty years. This interaction of time and place is usually shown by the dissolve. The dissolve acts as a "slower" transition, visually communicating to the viewer the fact of a major transition. Thus, the increase in the number of dissolves in this film.

The Nazis Strike, although basically an action film, utilized a great number of superimposures which dissolved into each other creating simultaneous montage (showing two or more images in a single frame).

The number of wipes in the films is quite large by present standards. The wipe was a popular method of breaking action or showing a time lapse during the 1930's and early 1940's. It was especially popular with Capra who used it extensively in his feature films. In the case of Prelude to War and War Comes to America, there was a great deal of change of place and time. In The Battle of Britain, the battle was told chronologically and thus there is a great deal of "minor" time change. The number of fades and irises is not unusual in any of the films.

Function. Each of the various elements of transition are used for a number of functions.

Cuts.--Cuts are used for the most part to create individual units depicting an action or event. For example, dog fights in The Battle of Britain are depicted by short strips of films joined by cuts. The Japanese assault on Manchuria is depicted by short and long strips again joined by cuts. The same process occurs throughout the films.

Because most of the individual sequences in the films are composed of a variety of visual material, there is little use of cuts to foster matching action (the technique of reshooting action that has taken place at the conclusion of the preceding shot; appropriate joining of the two shots results in a smooth flow of action which minimizes the disjunctiveness of juxtaposing two different fields of view). Few scenes were shot with two or more camera set-ups and thus matched continuity is infrequent. When it does occur, it is in the studio production scenes.

There are a few instances of jump cuts to facilitate shock. One occurs in War Comes to America, where a long shot of people sunning on a beach is followed by a CU of a dead American soldier lying on a beach. In Prelude to War, a shot of soldiers marching in a parade is followed by a shot of a burning ship at Pearl Harbor. In The Nazis Strike, a quick succession of shots of cannons firing follows a CU of Hitler. These instances, however, are relatively few. Even in most of these cases just mentioned, the visual cut is "softened" by a narrative or musical transition.

Fades.--Fades are used in the films only to mark significant breaks in action, place or time. The opening shot in each film always fades in from black. In Prelude to War, a fade is used to move from the free world to the slave world and vice versa. In War Comes to America, fast fades are used to bridge significant breaks in time and action. Outside of these instances, however, little use is made of them.

Dissolves.--Dissolves are used in all of the films and in several quite frequently. They perform several distinct functions.

Dissolves are not used to mark significant breaks in action or large time lapses. This function is performed for the most part by wipes, fades and irises. Dissolves are used for minor scene or time changes. For example, in Prelude to War, a shot of a Japanese general shaking hands with an official is followed by a newspaper headline stating, "Stimson denounces Jap Aggression." A dissolve is used between these two shots. Dissolves are used several times to "compress" time within a single sequence. In The Battle of Britain, a shot of a crew entering a bomber dissolves into the propeller starting. Also in The Battle of Britain, a shot of people sleeping in a shelter dissolves into a shot of a man coming out of a shelter in the morning. In War Comes to America, the events of November 26, 1941, are shown by a shot of the State Department building dissolving into Secretary of State Stimson speaking, this in turn dissolving into Japanese officials leaving the State Department building. There were no flashbacks or future time changes in the films.

The dissolve can also be used to slow down the action of a sequence and provide a dramatic pause. This function is found a number of times in the films. The shots which are dissolved do in all probability contain additional meaning. However, the dissolve as a transition between them acts as a dramatic pause. In Prelude to War, a shot of Mussolini talking is slowly dissolved into a map of Ethiopia, allowing the narrator time to reflect on Mussolini's words. In Divide and Conquer, a slow dissolve from a shot of rows of French soldiers to rows of white crosses adds an element of meaning otherwise not achieved by another form of transition. In War Comes to America, the last shot in a sequence showing American soldiers fighting dissolves slowly to a shot of the Statue of Liberty. Here the viewer has time to catch his mental breath before jumping into the next sequence. In The Battle of Britain, the last shot in a sequence depicting German equipment assembled for the invasion of England is slowly dissolved into an animation describing the German plan for invasion.

The greatest use of dissolves is to maintain contact between somewhat unrelated shots. A dissolve is often used in the films to connect two shots which are discontinuous in space. In other words, the film is referring to the same event or action but the locale changes. This is often employed in montage units depicting a particular action. In Prelude to War, the Nazi occupation of Paris is characterized by three shots--a Nazi flag flying on a pole, German boots marching and German troops marching through the Arc de Triumphe--all connected by dissolves. In The Nazis Strike, the Siegfried line is depicted by five separate shots all connected by dissolves. In The Battle of Britain, a shot of a plane flying dissolves into a shot of a pencil writing the location of the plane, which in turn dissolves back into the plane flying.

Another use of the dissolve in this general category is to connect smoothly two essentially unrelated shots which generally have some connection of meaning. In War Comes to America, a shot of Hitler dissolves in a statue of a swastika. The shots are unrelated visually, but have a strong connotative connection. In Prelude to War, a shot of a crowd applauding dissolves into a shot of church spires with Nazi flags flying over them. The crowd is applauding Dr. Alfred Rosenberg who is stating that the cross must be removed from the churches. This connection of meaning is carried over by the dissolve. In The Nazis Strike, three shots depicting the material wealth of Germany--shots of a maze of oil towers, logs rolling down a chute into a river and a steam shovel scooping out dirt--are connected by dissolves. Thus, three essentially unrelated shots are visually and connotatively connected through dissolves. In The Battle of Britain, a shot of bombs being loaded dissolves into a shot of an officer at a desk picking up a phone. The sequence involved is the Bremen raid, and thus two unrelated shots gain meaning through the dissolve.

Yet another use of the dissolve is to act as a transition between matching action, position or form. This is used frequently in the films, mostly to match position and form. This is most often used in maps and drawings to effect a smooth change. In The Nazis Strike, a drawing of the earth is shown in four shots with dissolves connecting the basic form while some of the information changes. In Prelude to War, a shot of one wall plaque dissolves into another while the writing on the plaques changes. In The Battle of Britain, two shots of Hitler and Goerring bending over a table are connected by dissolves.

All of these dissolve functions appear continually throughout the films. They are essentially designed to provide contact and coherence between shots. They smooth out what might be jolting transitions between unrelated shots. Also, they are used in several instances for no apparent reason other than to break up the pattern of a scene, though this does not occur often since the pace of the films is very deliberately controlled. In most instances there is a very definite reason for the dissolve. The major reasons have been given here.

As was noted earlier, dissolves are not usually used to effect significant breaks in time, place or action. This function is reserved for wipes and irises.

Wipes.--Wipes, especially, play a prominent part in Prelude to War. Within seven shots depicting different aspects of the depression in the United States there are four wipes. Each of them marks a major

change in time and locale. A swastika wipe is used several times in

Prelude to War to mark a change in scene from Germany to Japan and

Italy. In War Comes to America wipes in the form of the shadows of

German soldiers marching across the frame are employed. In a wipe a

perceptible line passes across the screen. In the instance here men-

tioned, the line is the back of the troops; again, the wipe is used

to bridge a major break in time. Seven consecutive wipes are used in

Prelude to War between shots of seven different Nazi leaders. The

effect here, rather than a break in time, is the grouping of the men

together. They all represent the same ideas and the wipes work to

produce an overpowering effect.

Irises.--Irises are employed very infrequently and always mark

a distinct change in locale or time. In War Comes to America, an iris

is evolved out of the outlines of a drawing of Italy, Germany and

Japan. Each iris opens out of the outline of the country to reveal

"live" footage. This is the only distinctive use of the iris, although

all of the films except Divide and Conquer, and The Battle of Russia

contain them.

Transitions in the "Why We Fight" films employ a variety of forms

and perform several distinct functions. For the most part, the transi-

tions are objective and designed to produce continuity and move the

spectator along. Only infrequently are they used for subjective inter-

pretation. They, like camera and lens angle, are employed realistically

to present information as clearly and concisely as possible.

Length of Shot

    Use. Length of shot plays an important role in the establishment of pace and rhythm in the films. The following table provides some basic data on shot length. The total length of the films and the average and individual shot lengths are recorded in feet and frames.

TABLE VI

	Total Shots	Total length (ft.+frames)	Average shot length (ft.+frames)	Shortest shot (frames)	Longest shot (ft.+frames)
Prelude to War	774	1798+30	2	1	24+32
The Nazis Strike	637	1393+4	2+8	11	32+34
Divide and Conquer	1046	1998	1+36	3	65
The Battle of Britain	1099	1772+36	1+24	8	60
The Battle of Russia	1600	7363	4+24	8	81
War Comes to America	1406	2300+23	1+24	2	29.5

The average length of all shots in the films, with the exception of The Battle of China, is 2/5, or 3.5 seconds at sound film speed. Richard Byrne, in his study of German expressionistic films, stated regarding shot length that it is difficult to place the German films in their proper stylistic perspective, since comparable figures are not available for other film genres.[7] This still remains the case except for his study. In comparing German expressionist films with the "Why We Fight" films, it is found that the average cutting rate of the "Why We Fight" films is almost twice the speed of the German expressionist films. Comparison of these two styles still does not reveal a great deal that is meaningful, however. The two series of films were in entirely different styles and the German films were, of course, silent. This fact alone makes the comparison somewhat meaningless.

Function. Despite the difficulty of comparing the "Why We Fight" films with other films with exactitude, it is apparent that the average cutting rate is rapid. However, the pace is not pell-mell. The films tend to set up a piece of action or an event and then proceed to reveal it in a series of shots that are fairly short and move in rapid sequence. Throughout the films a cutting pattern of a long shot followed by a number of short shots depicting the scene or action is apparent. In Divide and Conquer, especially, this pattern recurs with regularity. A long shot, usually an animation, sets the scene for the invasion of one of the Low Countries. This is followed by a series of relatively short shots depicting the invasion. The content of a sequence is shown by a series of shots which follow each other in rapid succession and build up the image of attack. This pattern occurs in all the films, although not with any special rhythmic pattern.

There is not, with possibly four exceptions, any distinct rhythmical pattern in the films. That the pace of the films is rapid is readily observable. It might be supposed from this rapid pace that there is a discernible rhythm as well. There is a great deal of difference between speed and rhythm in film. The "Why We Fight" series has a characterizable speed, but no distinct rhythm.

There are to be sure some sequences where long strips of film work to create a quiet rhythm or where short strips create a quick rhythm. However, these are interspersed at random through the films

and do not form part of any overall rhythmic pattern. In The Nazis
Strike, long shots do help to establish a quiet rhythm in the sequence
showing Polish dead. In The Battle of Britain, long shots establish a
quiet rhythm, in the sequence showing the death and destruction at
Coventry.

The short shots in the film do not really establish a quick rhythm.
Many elements hinder this process, including the frequent use of supers,
titles and the contrary pace of the narrator.

The only true rhythmic cutting in the entire series occurs in War
Comes to America. The sequence begins with shot 164 and concludes with
shot 240. The sequence depicts the material growth of the United
States. Shots of railroad ties being laid, telephone wires being
strung, herds of cattle, ships, harvesters cutting grain, oil gushing
from derricks, molten steel pouring from a vat, steam shovels scooping
up the earth, water pouring from a dam, bridges being built--among
other shots--are skillfully cut to establish a basic pattern of rhythm.
The entire sequence is backed by the song "Rhapsody in Blue." The
shots are cut to the tempo of this song. They are all one-half second
(12 frames), one second (24 frames) or two seconds (48 frames) long.
Fifty of the seventy-five shots are one second long. The half-second
and two-second shots are intercut to coincide with the change in rhythm
of the song. Thus, the growth of the material wealth of the United
States is characterized by a fast driving rhythm. Shot moves into shot
and the sequence builds and carries the viewer along. At specific
points, shots are held for two seconds or a half-second and then the
basic one-second rhythm is re-established. The sequence ends with a

long (144 frames) tracking aerial shot of a semi-completed Empire State Building against a New York skyline. Thus, as the song reaches its climax, the peak of American material achievement is shown.

The only other instance where some degree of rhythmic cutting is evident is in the sequence in War Comes to America depicting the food Americans consume. The music again establishes the fast tempo and the shots pick up the rhythm. The shots are not as perfectly timed as in the previously mentioned sequence. Fast motion within the shots also helps to establish the rapid mood. The shots start out at twenty-five to thirty-five frames long and are gradually shortened as the tempo picks up, finally ending up with seven- and eight-frame shots.

This lack of rhythm is caused by several elements. The most important is the narration, which,as was noted previously, plays a dominant role in the films. The necessity to coincide the visuals with the narration hinders and in most cases destroys any attempt at rhythmic cutting, as most of the narration had little distinct rhythm. It is notable that where even slight rhythmic patterns emerge, the narration is absent.

However, other elements also work to destroy rhythm in the films. The simple necessity to see content hinders rhythm. An important shot may have to be held for insertion of dialogue. The great amount of camera movement necessitates for the most part longer shots and thus the definite establishment of a rhythmic pattern is here, too, hindered. The frequent use of titles and the necessity for the viewer and/or the narrator to read them disrupts rhythmic patterns. The frequent use of supers and wipes and irises also hinders rhythm. Supers necessitate a

longer shot because of the double visual content and thus this tends
to break up any rhythmic patterns.

Once again, the need to present information clearly and completely
dominates the concept of rhythm and shot length in the films. The basic
concern with shot length is understanding and not cinematic effect.
Thus, if shot length and rhythm can aid in the presentation of information, all well and good. If they cannot, they must be and are sacrificed.

Editing

Editing in this analysis refers to the pattern in which shots are
assembled, the pattern which the individual scenes and sequences take
on in the films.

It must be realized that all the elements previously mentioned
form a part of the editing pattern, especially transition and length
of shot. However, it is the particular way in which these elements
are used to portray a scene or sequence that is under consideration now.

The basic editing pattern that emerges from the films is one of
many shots in combination working to communicate the meaning of a
sequence. There is a basic pattern in the films whereby the narration coupled with a title, an animation or a series of long shots sets
a scene. Then, the visuals are allowed to take over and carry the
sense of the scene. The ways in which the message of a sequence is
communicated is not by one or two long shots with a great deal of explanation, but by a succession of shots which function to build up an
image of the idea being communicated. This editing pattern is not
Eisenstein's dialectical montage. Rather, the editing pattern is
likened more to Pudovkin's concept of montage. Pudovkin's pattern of

editing is that of a director dissecting an unbroken scene into component parts, into elements,and then selecting from them sparingly those
shots which render the essence of the scene.[8] This is the basic pattern
of editing that emerges in the "Why We Fight" films. Depiction of the
battle for Poland or France, for example, is not by a continuous pattern
of time-related shots following the action and utilizing a great deal
of matched action. Rather, it is depicted by selected shots which build
up the essence of the battle. Crosscuttihg between German tanks and
Polish cavalry, shot after shot showing the different elements of the
German blitz, all work to produce the image of conquest. The air
battles in The Battle of Britain are not depicted through extreme
long tracking shots with the narrator guiding the viewer along. The
image of the battle is built upon a succession of selected shots which
create the essence of the battle.

This building pattern is achieved in two ways. One is by using
shots as in a mosaic to present a picture of war. Shots are inserted
piece by piece to make up the pattern of the mosaic. The second
method is by presenting a scene or sequence in a form of rough continuity of time. There is no mosaic here; rather, the action is
depicted more or less continuously as it occurs in time. The first
use is by far the dominant pattern in the films. There is little concern for true continuity in the films. This mosaic pattern emerges
most consistently in the "action" films such as The Nazis Strike,
Divide and Conquer, The Battle of Britain and The Battle of Russia.

There is one other basic form of editing in the films. This
particular form appears almost exclusively in Prelude to War and War

Comes to America. These two films are somewhat more complicated than
the others in that they deal with the flow of history and the various
elements within three different societies that combined to produce war.
There is relatively little straight action sequences in these films.
Rather, editing works here to establish interrelationships between
events and especially between the three Axis powers as contrasted to
America. Here, the basic editing pattern is the establishing of a
space relation. Frequent intercutting between the three Axis powers
is characteristic of this pattern. The most striking element in this
pattern is the economical and rapid intercutting between the Axis
powers. The idea that the three powers are alike in their philosophies
and ambitions to rule the world through conquest is shown by quick
movement between sequences. Slow dissolves and fades might hinder
this flow. Wipes and cuts do establish the relationship. Prelude to
War is almost in the form of a three-way counterpoint among the Axis
powers. Themes such as children, as discussed in Chapter IV, are presented across all three powers with clearness and conciseness. There
is a steady movement from one power to another. The spectator is
prodded by the films and made to keep pace. The viewer is rarely
allowed to set his own pace.

Thus the editing pattern, like all of the elements of film construction is used to facilitate the presentation of information in a
clear, concise manner. Yet the pattern of editing is never boring or
pedantic. It is an impelling driving pattern that quickly build up
images and moves the spectator on. Editing is used to present ideas
and information in a clear yet visually impressive and compelling way.

It never gets in the way of the true purpose of the films, to present information and reasons to the soldier about why he is fighting.

SUMMARY

Some attempt should be made to characterize each individual film or at least groups of them. There were certain differences in approach and style in all the films. But, as a whole, the films retained a remarkable degree of stylistic unity. Each film utilized the elements of filmic construction in slightly different ways to facilitate the particular subject it was treating. Films such as The Nazis Strike, Divide and Conquer, The Battle of Russia and The Battle of Britain are action oriented films. They portray a relatively limited arena of time and space. Thus, these films treat individual topics, battles or events much more thoroughly than similar events are treated in Prelude to War or War Comes to America. Scenes are built carefully rather than just being highlighted. A good example of this occurs in The Nazis Strike and War Comes to America, involving scenes depicting a Nazi rally in Madison Square Garden. The same rally is shown, but in The Nazis Strike, the scene is revealed in nine separate shots totaling 18/7. In War Comes to America, the same scene is treated in five shots encompassing 11/12. Prelude to War and War Comes to America cover twenty years of history in four separate countries. Thus, they do not concentrate on portraying the action of a battle. Nor do they place as much emphasis upon maintaining a steady forward-moving pace. Rather, they move more slowly, moving laterally as well as forward. Thus, more time is devoted to explanation and summary than in the other four

films. Little time is left for the spectator to reflect on the events
portrayed in The Battle of Russia, The Battle of Britain, Divide and
Conquer and The Nazis Strike; nor is there much need to do so. The
films convey battles and action. What summaries are needed are generally included at the end of the films.

All of the elements of film construction are employed essentially
for one basic purpose--the clear and understandable presentation of
information. The films are essentially tools of teaching utilized to
convey more effectively the reasons behind the war and why the individual soldier was in uniform. There was little use of the elements of
visual style for symbolic purposes.

If one single element could be singled out as contributing most
to the films sense of visual style, it would be editing. The basic
construction of the films depended upon the building characteristics
of a variety of shots. Continuous action of a battle from a camera
boom was not available. Certain isolated and often unrelated shots
were sometimes all that was available. Thus, there was little control
over the basic elements of film construction (camera angle, lens angle,
lighting, etc.) so common to all film. The impressiveness of the films
could not rest on a distinctive lighting pattern, a picturesque set or
acting. These elements upon which so much of film depends for meaning
and interpretation were, for the most part, denied the makers of the
"Why We Fight" series. As Richard Griffith stated concerning the "Why
We Fight" films,

> Deprived of star glamour and production value,
> drawing their material from newsreel archives
> and combat film photographed at random on the

fighting fronts, they were forced back upon the
basic resources of the film medium; the editing
principle emerged as the definitive factor in
the conception and execution of every film.[9]

FOOTNOTES - CHAPTER VI

[1]Charles R. Reynolds, Jr., "The Use of Motion Picture Techniques
n Live Dramatic Television Productions" (unpublished Masters thesis,
niversity of Michigan, 1956), pp. 13-147.

[2]Rudolf Arnheim, Film as Art (Berkeley: University of California
ress, 1964), p. 38.

[3]Memorandum, National Archives, Washington D.C., "Why We Fight"
eries file.

[4]C. I. Hovland, A. A. Lumsdaine, and F. D. Sheffield, Experiments
n Mass Communication (New York: John Wiley & Sons, Inc., 1965), p. 90.

[5]Ibid.

[6]Richard Byrne, personal analyses of German expressionistic films,
ichard Byrne, University of Texas, Austin, Texas.

[7]Richard Byrne, "German Cinematic Expressionism: 1919-1924"
unpublished Ph.D. dissertation, State University of Iowa, 1962), p. 313.

[8]V. I. Pudovkin, "The Plastic Material," in Film: A Montage of
heories, ed. by Richard Dyer MacCann (New York: E. P. Dutton & Co.,
nc., 1966), p. 33.

[9]Paul Rotha and Richard Griffith, The Film Till Now (London:
pring Books, 1967), pp. 461-62.

233

SUMMARY AND DISCUSSION

BASIC FOCUS OF STUDY

This study is an historical and descriptive analysis of the "Why
We Fight" series. The research focused on two areas of analysis. The
first involved describing the evolution and development of the documentary film, both military and civilian, during wartime. Included
within this area were a description of the evolution of the Army's concern about morale and a history and description of the "Why We Fight"
series itself.

The second area's attention is focused on the films themselves.
There were seven films in the series: (1) Prelude to War, (2) The Nazis
Strike, (3) Divide and Conquer, (4) The Battle of Britain, (5) The Battle
of Russia, (6) The Battle of China, (7) War Comes to America. These
films were thematically and structurally analyzed and described. The
structural analysis examined the sound track and visual style of the
films.

SUMMARY AND DISCUSSION

History

World War I saw the first confrontation between the documentary
film and war. The main thrust of the documentary movement in World
War I was civilian through the Committee of Public Information headed

234

by George Creel. The CPI formed its own bureau of films and produced
a number of different films. The most well-known and popular were the
three feature-length films, <u>Pershing's Crusaders</u>, <u>America's Answer</u> and
<u>Under Four Flags</u>. The basic concern in the World War I civilian docu-
mentary was in selling the war and America to the American public. The
films of the CPI (either produced by it or for it) were designed to
"advertise" the qualities of American life and instill desire in the
American public to pitch in and "get it over with over there."

The military use of film was somewhat limited; only sixty-two
films were made. The films were all essentially instructional films.
The end of the war saw much of the Army's film activity curtailed.
Little was done regarding documentary film production by the Army
(specifically the Signal Corps) until the middle 1930's. Then with
the beginning of the American documentary film movement in 1936 and
growing international tensions, some effort was made to initiate a
stronger film program within the Signal Corps. The first peacetime
draft brought much of the debate concerning an Army film program to a
close. With the influx of thousands of untrained men into the Army,
the need for a faster means to train and educate them became acute.

At the same time, the Army was becoming aware of the need for
films, the civilian documentary effort was being aided by the United
States government. The formation of the U. S. Film Service in 1939
was the peak of the prewar civilian documentary effort.

With the advent of war in December, 1941, both the civilian and
military use of film grew tremendously. The main thrust of civilian
wartime documentary was centered in the Office of War Information and

the Coordinator of Inter-American Affairs. Both agencies produced and distributed documentaries. The OWI, after a brief try at producing its own films, was basically a distributor of military and civilian films. The CIAA produced films for Latin and South American consumption.

The military story of documentary film is essentially the story of the Signal Corps. While the Navy, Air Force and the Marines utilized films extensively, and engaged in the production and distribution of many films, it was the Army Signal Corps (specifically the Army Pictorial Service) that was the key factor in military film production during World War II.

Most military film activity resulted in the production of training films. They were used for every conceivable purpose and instructional need the Army had. Another important aspect of the Signal Corps' film work involved the production of orientation films, which included the "Why We Fight" series. Other important film activities included the production of historical campaign films, such as John Ford's The Battle of Midway, the "Army-Navy Screen Magazine," produced by Leonard Spigelgass, industry-incentive films produced for civilian war factory workers, "Staff Reports," "Combat Bulletins," and a chronology of the war.

In summary, it should be noted that it was World War II that was basically responsible for the great growth in both civilian and military quarters, of films for purposes of education. It can also be concluded in agreement with Richard Griffith that most of the film activity in World War II fell outside of the scope of true documentary.[1] Most of the films produced during World War II were instructional in nature. They were not social statements designed to convince; however, this is not to demean them.

Two concepts above all characterize the film effort in World War II: variety and scope. Film was used for every conceivable need in World War II. It taught, informed, persuaded and entertained. It performed these tasks on a scale never before or since duplicated. At the Army's peak, there was a nightly audience of over 1,900,000.[2] At the end of the war there was a library of over 13,500,000 feet of uncut film.[3]

The documentary film in World War II above all reflected the tradition that had preceded it. There were few radical changes in style or purpose. What made the effort truly significant was the number of needs which were served by film and the scope of the operation set up to meet these needs.

Thus, the "Why We Fight" series was but one program in a huge and varied operation. This one series, however, was important not only in itself and its personal achievement, but also for what it reflected concerning the Army's attitude toward the morale of the individual soldier.

Prior to World War II, there had been little concern in the Army about morale in terms of soldier motivation and stimulation. However, with the influx of thousands of "unwilling volunteers" in 1940, the Army was faced with an attitude problem. It soon became apparent that morale involved more than recreation and amusement. Volleyball and good food were not especially strong motivating factors to the average draftee. Something more was needed.

Thus, in 1941, several factors, including the stimulus of public interest and criticism and the growing unrest in an expanding Army, produced an expansion in Morale Branch activity to include mental stimulation and training.

With the onset of war in December, 1941, the need for attitude formation and information as to why the United States was at war became acute. Out of this need for attitude formation on a mass level came the "Why We Fight" series. The top priority placed on these films made it clear that the Army realized that orientation was all important and that the "why" of the war had to be communicated just as urgently as the "how."

The "Why We Fight" series was designed to implement the overall orientation program of the Army. An indication of its value is that the films of the series were required viewing by all troops before going overseas, the fact of viewing being marked on the individual soldier's record.

The films themselves were made with remarkable speed (approximately one every five months) and almost entirely by Hollywood-trained personnel. Frank Capra was the key figure in the series. It was he who gave the films their basic idea and form.

This fact, that the men responsible for the creation and production of the "Why We Fight" series were almost all Hollywood commercial motion picture trained personnel, is perhaps the single most "outstanding" historical fact concerning the series. These men demonstrated the adaptability, versatility and film intelligence of the true film artist. Whether it was Capra, Litvak or Hornbeck editing the films, Veiller and Knight writing the scripts or Tiomkin composing and conducting the music, they were all able to "break the mold" and adapt to meet the needs of the time. That they were able to do so is also a reflection on the strong tradition and influence of the documentary film in the United States prior to the war. Capra and his crew had no previous documentary experience, so they turned to "examples" such as The River, The Plow That Broke the Plains and "The March of Time," among others, for inspiration and information on techniques.

Thus, the "Why We Fight" series was historically a meeting of the talent of a commercial industry, a strong tradition of documentary film used for social statement and the needs of war. All of these elements interacted to produce what most critics acknowledge were the finest films to emerge from World War II.

Themes

An analysis of the "Why We Fight" films reveals several obvious themes. Nine separate themes were isolated. (1) The people, (2) religion, (3) children, (4) historical tradition, (5) hatred of war, (6) leaders, (7) slavery-machines, (8) courage and intelligence of the allies, and (9) the allies' buying time for the world. These individual themes were presented within the two general frameworks of explication and contrast.

Each of the themes is presented in a factual way. There seems to exist within the films a desire to "prove" the themes. They are, therefore, not just stated or tossed out to the viewer to be understood, believed or accepted. All of the themes are "backed up" with information in the form of statistics, quotes, charts, maps, etc. The concept that children in the countries conquered by the Axis powers are killed and beaten is not merely stated; it is visually demonstrated. This demonstration occurs essentially through the narration and the visuals. All of the themes receive the same emphasis.

Frequently, contrast is used to characterize themes, particularly the attempts to contrast a "free world" with a "slave world." Each of the themes is basically a value or characteristic of one of the two worlds. Religion, for example, is emphasized as a basic characteristic of the free world; irreligiousness of the slave world.

There is little that is new or different with respect to the themes of the films. Five of them (the people, religion, children, historical tradition, hatred of war) are essentially traditional values of the free world, particularly the United States. These themes are basically emotional in nature, but are still presented within an explication framework. The films do not just state that these are values and characteristics of a free society, but attempt to prove that they are.

The same is true of the two themes which characterize the slave world, leaders and slavery-machines. The slave world is depicted in terms of leaders--Hitler, Mussolini and Hirohito. The people of the Axis countries are only shown being "taken in" by these men. The machine emphasis is often depicted by film of tank treads crossing in front of the camera or superimposed over dead bodies to symbolize the Axis conquest of a country.

There are two basically rational themes (courage and intelligence of the allies, and the allies' buying time for the world) which are emphasized in the "ally" films, The Battle of Britain, The Battle of Russia and The Battle of China. These are themes which require demonstration. They are designed to "build up" America's fighting allies in the minds of the American soldier.

The themes are expressed primarily through the narration with visual duplication of the statements. However, there are several instances where the visuals alone convey the theme (they often are used to depict Nazi brutality to children).

The themes are simple, to the point and repeated. All of the basic filmic elements such as narration, music, natural sounds and visuals are utilized to convey the themes. The themes are usually duplicated across filmic elements rather than through only a single element. The themes are not merely to be understood, they are to be accepted. Thus, they are simple, explicit and presented in duplication across both sound and sight. Persuasive and informative subtlety was a luxury the Army could not afford. The themes do answer the question, "Why do we fight?" They answer it clearly and with force.

Sound

The sound track of the "Why We Fight" films consists of speech, natural sound effects and music. All three elements performed a variety of tasks.

Narration was the most dominant element of the sound track. The major narration for all the films was done by Anthony Veiller and Walter Huston; on occasion, several other voices appeared. The two men differed somewhat in their style of speaking. Huston's voice seems raspy and older than Veiller's. Huston is semi-dramatic, even-paced and very definitely low key. His voice is fairly heavy and filled with authority. Veiller's voice is more high-pitched and "biting" in quality. He is most often used when the films take on a definite

instructional tone. His voice is more intense and driving than Huston's.
Both of the voices were not "dramatic" and did not have or assume the
characteristics of the standard "voice-of-God" narrator.

The narration is used for a number of tasks. It builds up tension,
it punctuates the visuals and most of all it sets scenes and explains
events and actions in detail. The narration, more than any other single
film element aids comprehension and makes the ideas and concepts the
films are trying to communicate easily understood. To do this the
narration needed to function on the level of the audience it was addres-
sing. Thus, the main stylistic element of the narration is that it is
colloquial. It is even slangy. It spoke to the troops in a language
and on a level they could comprehend. The narration is perhaps, by
modern standards, over-used and simple. However, it rarely stands out;
rather, it blends in with the visuals and the other sound elements to
create a total film statement.

Natural sound is another sound element in the films. Here, the
sounds of war, of crowds yelling, of factories in the middle of production, etc., help to create the reality of the films and aid in
establishing atmosphere. Natural sound is not merely used to duplicate
the visuals, but is used plastically to create audio images of events
and action.

Music is the third element of the sound track. It consists of a
variety of elements including full orchestra, singing chorus, solo
instrument and solo voice. The main function of the music is to aid
in establishing the emotional quality in the films. It also aids in
establishing the atmosphere in a scene. Tiomkin, the composer of the

scores for the films, said that he composed for emotion.[4] Scenes
depicting action have fast-paced, exciting music. Scenes showing the
suffering of the civilian population of countries conquered by the
Axis powers utilize somber music to add to and convey the pathos of
the events.

The music is very literal and simple. It is always appropriate
to the visuals and has immediate appeal. Extensive use is made of well-
known songs to aid the immediacy of musical comprehension. The music,
as with the narration and natural sounds, rarely stands out or calls
attention to itself. It blends in with the other film elements to
create a complete filmic statement.

In summary, the sound track of the "Why We Fight" series is not
merely "window-dressing." The slabs of visual fact which form the
basic structure of the compilation form need placement, emphasis and
above all interpretation. Rarely can the visuals stand alone. They
often require explanation and interpretation to be understood. They
often require emotion to create an impact. Much of the force and
understanding of the films comes through the sound track and its relationship to the visual elements of the films.

Visual Style

Eight visual elements,which uniformly are considered as consti-
tuting film style, were isolated and analyzed. They are: (1) camera
angle, (2) lens angle, (3) camera movement, (4) content, (5) optical
variations, (6) transitions, (7) length of shot, and (8) editing.
These elements are basic to all film construction. It is how they
are used that gives them a certain style and characteristics.

All of the visual elements without exception are employed for one basic purpose--to aid understanding, to present as clear a picture of an idea, action or event as possible. This function is not surprising. The compilation form is composed for the most part of film that was shot for another purpose and not specifically for the film in which it is being used. Thus, most of the footage for the "Why We Fight" series is newsreel and combat film. The original intent of most of the footage, especially with the newsreel and combat film, was to convey the content of an action or event as clearly as possible. Most of the footage was shot "on-the-spot" as it occurred. There could be no re-takes to "correct" the camera angle, lens angle or lighting or to alter it for a different viewpoint.

Thus, the basic function of camera angle, lens angle, camera movement, optical variations, lighting and setting is to convey the content of a sequence as clearly as possible. The main objective is to aid the viewer in understanding the action or event being shown. Ever superimpositions, which are normally used in commercial enter-tainment motion pictures to create a sense of chaos and confusion, are used in the "Why We Fight" films to show the similarity of meaning between two objects in one shot. Two elements of content, titles and animations, are employed frequently to aid understanding.

There are, to be sure, instances where "intra-shot" elements are used for symbolic comment or suggestion, but these are by far the "minor" functions employed in these elements.

It is the "inter-shot" elements of transition, shot length and especially editing that give the "Why We Fight" series its distinctive visual style. Economy is a key characteristic of the use of these elements. Transitions are used mainly to move the spectator's eye. They aid in the establishing of pace in the films. Shot length also helps to move the viewer along at the film's pace. There is little true rhythm in the films, because the pace of the narrator, the use of titles and animations hinders an establishment of a definite rhythm.

Editing is the key element in the visual structure of the films. Editing is, of course, a combination of most of the elements of filmic construction, but the stress in editing is placed upon the assembly of the shots into a specific, meaningful pattern.

The editing pattern assumes two basic forms. The first is a mosaic where an event or action is communicated by selecting various phases and pieces of an action or event and assembling them into a complete picture. The assembly is usually not in any continuous pattern; rather, events are selected which best interpret the nature of a scene. These events or actions are at times juxtaposed; at times a rough form of continuity is presented. However, the end result is a complete picture.

The other basic pattern of editing is counterpoint. This pattern is especially prevalent in <u>Prelude to War</u> and <u>War Comes to America</u>, where the events of twenty years across four nations are presented. The film may present a theme, such as children, and then through editing, cut across four countries revealing the nature of the nation's children and each country's philosophy toward them. The editing pattern here basically functions to combine the countries according to theme and yet keep them separate in the viewers' minds. Thus, a mosaic pattern is used in establishing a concept or event within a country or limited area of time or place; the larger counterpoint pattern assembles these mosaics and communicates them to the audience. The key element here, too, is economy. The films do not waste time in meticulously building up a scene or theme; rather, as in Pudovkin's concept of editing, only those shots which best illustrate the event or action are used. Thus, the pace of the films is rapid. The films prod the spectator and bombard him with visuals, which taken individually do not communicate a great deal, but when assembled into a definite pattern, communicate the meaning of a scene or sequence.

Thus, the "Why We Fight" films do not exhibit many of the normal visual elements which are used to communicate a message--acting, setting, camera angle, etc. Yet the meaning of the messages in the "Why We Fight" films is communicated. The key element in this communication is editing. Because of selection of only those shots which best illustrate the action or event (even though often limited in choice) and their combination into fast moving individual patterns, the films communicate information in a clear, understandable and yet compelling way.

Final Conclusions

Richard MacCann has stated that the "Why We Fight" films were a combination of a sermon, a between halves pep talk and a barroom bull session.[5] This is not, in this writer's opinion, an accurate characterization. To be sure, there are certain elements of the film which have the quality of a sermon, a pep talk or a bull session. The narration more than any other element perhaps conveys these characteristics.

However, the films are carefully designed and structured and thus do not really fit MacCann's characterization. In all fairness to Mr. MacCann, it should be pointed out that his comment is being used at this point in the study as a starting point in the critical examination of the series. Also, his observation was based upon a normal viewing experience and not on any intensive analysis.

The films are effective teaching devices and "good" film. This is a combination that is difficult to achieve. The films did convey information to the troops--so effectively, in fact, that a majority of the men tested in research conducted on the film's effectiveness remembered the correct answers to questions six months later.[6] The films are also visually interesting and compelling. They are recognized by film theorists and critics as films of high artistic quality. They, unlike the standard instructional and training films, not only communicated information, but communicated information in a compelling and vital manner.

One of the keys to this compelling manner may well be variety. Rarely is the burden of communicating a message left to one filmic element (in most documentary films this is the narration). Rather than being a visual duplication of every word the narrator states, the film elements interact and blend to produce a total film statement. The visuals form the basic material for the films' construction. Here are slabs of fact, shot in a variety of contexts. The editing pattern assembles them into coherent sequences, and sound functions to aid and/or establish their meaning and interpretation.

That the films were intended to persuade as well as inform--and did persuade in a few instances--is an accepted fact. It has not been the purpose of this study to analyze the films rhetorically as persuasive instruments. This is the subject of separate research by itself. That the films generally failed as persuasion is well documented. Certain reasons can be suggested--an apparent lack of clear cut persuasive objectives, the nature and limitation of the testing and the "civilian" predisposition of the men themselves.

Although the "Why We Fight" series' effectiveness as propaganda is questionable, its transformation of cold, unrelated slabs of fact into something exciting and appealing, communicating information to a large mass of men, is perhaps its distinctive quality as a film series.

The films' attempt at persuasion was persuasion by facts. The facts were usually allowed to speak for themselves. Very few conclusions were drawn for the audience. This "facts produce opinions, opinions produce attitudes" theorem was not especially successful. Perhaps here, the makers of the films overrated the capacity or basic orientation of their audience.

What are the characteristic elements and qualities of the "Why We Fight" series and how do they function as elements of filmic construction? The "Why We Fight" series used all the commonly recognized and applied elements of film construction. The eight elements which are basic to the construction of the films in the series have been set forth and described in detail. These elements are grouped into two separate categories, "intra-shot" elements and "inter-shot" elements.

Those elements within the shot (camera angle, lens angle, camera movement, content, optical variations) basically function to convey information. There is very little symbolic or interpretative use of these elements in the films. They are used to communicate the information and content within a particular shot.

It is the inter-shot elements and sound, however, which give the films much of their distinctive quality. The most distinctive quality, the one element which creates the basic format of the films and most effectively characterizes their style, is editing and the patterns it assumes. Building up mosaics of events and action and interrelating these across space and time resulted in examples of the compilation form at its best. Sound, particularly the narration and music, blended with the visual structure to clarify, explain and interpret. Capra and his men were, for the most part, denied conscious control over many of the elements of filmic construction; they were forced to rely primarily on editing and sound to communicate their particular message. The original reality of the shots was a reality that in many cases was different from what Capra and his men wanted to communicate. The use of editing and sound to interpret, explain and in some cases to "twist" the filmic elements to their own advantage, to create their own reality, made the films meaningful, understandable and compelling. The pace of the films was rapid, forcing the spectator to keep up. The films bombarded him with visuals which were formed into mosaics of action and events. These mosaics were often linked by a larger counterpoint pattern of editing along with music and a running narration.

To repeat, the "Why We Fight" films were effective teaching devices and artistic films. This combination makes them unique even in 1968.

LIMITATIONS OF THE STUDY

There are perhaps three limitations of this study. The first is an historical limitation. There was a very distinct lack of historical data on the "Why We Fight" series. Most of the World War II records of the series have either been destroyed or misplaced. Therefore, interviews were planned with several key personnel involved with the series. However, several of these individuals declined to make themselves available and thus, there are some elements of the history of the series as well as some insights into the construction of the films themselves which are perhaps unavoidably missing.

The second limitation of the study is minor--the unavailability of The Battle of China for detailed shot analysis. The film was viewed a number of times at the National Archives and it could be observed that it seemed to fall into the basic pattern of the other films, especially The Battle of Russia. A shot analysis would have made the study complete, even if it may have added little that was new or different.

A third limitation is the lack of information concerning the films' audience and its composition. This is certainly not a major limitation since the purpose of this study was to analyze the films themselves, not how they affected their audience. However, more information would have aided the evaluative portions of the study by enabling the researcher to point out why certain techniques were used and how well they functioned. It was at times difficult to maintain proper historical perspective concerning certain aspects of the films, especially when the exact nature of the audience for whom they were made was not accurately known.

IMPLICATIONS FOR FURTHER RESEARCH

There are essentially four directions which further research could take. By far, the most important direction is for further shot analysis studies to be made on other forms and styles of documentary film--indeed, all types of films. As Richard Byrne noted and this writer concurs, the data involving tabulation and measurement needs to be placed in some sort of perspective. When shot analyses of other films, particularly documentaries, are completed, the sections of this study utilizing detailed shot analysis will become more valuable. Perhaps in this way some answer to the question of what documentary film is can be arrived at.

A second direction for further research involves the films as communication. The films could be analyzed rhetorically as persuasive messages. This study in itself could take several directions. The Aristotelian principles of persuasion could be applied to the films to see how they functioned as persuasion in a "classical" sense. The films could also be analyzed in terms of several of the newer models of mass communication, such as that of MacLean and Westley, to see how they function in the total process of mass communication. The "Why We Fight" films were originally a series of lectures delivered by orientation officers. An interesting study might be to analyze the transformation of a persuasive argument from the medium of lecture to the medium of film.

A third area of further research is in the general area of the entire World War II film program. The entire program of the Signal Corps or the Navy as well as the OWI and the CIAA has never been treated in detail. Also separate aspects of the programs such as the historical campaign films of Wyler and Huston and the "Army-Navy Screen Magazine" could be analyzed.

A fourth area of further research involves those films which are currently being done concerning Vietnam and those films which were made during the Korean conflict. In both instances, films resembling the "Why We Fight" series in purpose (orientation and information) have been produced. An historical study involving a comparison of the films across three wars would be an interesting and valuable study.

FOOTNOTES - CHAPTER VII

[1]Paul Rotha, Sinclair Road, and Richard Griffith, Documentary Film (New York: Hastings House, 1963), p. 358.

[2]Orton Hicks, "Army Pictures Reach 'Round the World," Business Screen, VII (1945), p. 53.

[3]Edward Munson, Jr., "The Army Pictorial Service," Business Screen, VII (1945), p. 33.

[4]Dimitri Tiomkin, private telephone interview, October, 1967.

[5]Richard MacCann, "Documentary Film and Democratic Government: An Administrative History from Pare Lorentz to John Huston" (unpublished Ph.D. dissertation, Harvard, 1951), p. 349.

[6]C. I. Hovland, A. A. Lumsdaine, and F. D. Sheffield, Experiments on Mass Communication (New York: John Wiley & Sons, Inc., 1965), p. 64.

BIBLIOGRAPHY

Books

Agee, James. <u>Agee on Film</u>. Ed. by McDowell Obolensky. New York: McDowell Obolensky, Inc., 1958.

Alicoate, Jack, ed. <u>The Film Daily Yearbook</u>. Hollywood: The Film Daily, 1944.

Arnheim, Rudolf. <u>Film as Art</u>. Berkeley: University of California Press, 1958.

Baddeley, W. Hugh. <u>The Technique of Documentary Film Production</u>. New York: Hastings House, 1963.

Bluem, William A. <u>Documentary in American Television</u>. New York: Hastings House, 1965.

Buchanan, Andrew. <u>The Film in Education</u>. London: Phoenix House, Ltd., 1951.

Creel, George. <u>How We Advertised America</u>. New York: Harper and Brothers, 1920.

"Frank Capra." <u>Current Biography</u>. New York: H. W. Wilson Co., 1948.

Griffith, Richard. <u>Frank Capra</u>. London: The British Film Institute, n.d.

Herman, Lewis. <u>Educational Films</u>. New York: Crown Publishers, Inc., 1965.

Hoban, Charles. <u>Movies That Teach</u>. New York: Dryden Press, 1946.

Hovland, C. I., Lumsdaine, A. A. and Sheffield, F. D. <u>Experiments on Mass Communication</u>. New York: John Wiley & Sons., Inc., 1965.

Knight, Arthur. <u>The Liveliest Art</u>. New York: The Macmillan Co., 1957.

Kracauer, Siegfried. <u>From Caligari to Hitler; A Psychological Study of the German Film</u>. Princeton: Princeton University Press, 1947.

_____. <u>Theory of Film; The Redemption of Physical Reality</u>. New York: Oxford University Press, 1960.

Leyda, Jay. Films Beget Films. New York: Hill and Wang, 1964.

Manvell, Roger, and Huntley, John. The Technique of Film Music. London: Focal Press, Ltd., 1957.

Marshall-Calder, Arthur. The Innocent Eye. London: W. H. Allen, 1963.

Nilsen, Vladimir. The Cinema as a Graphic Art: On a Theory of Representation in the Cinema. Translated by Stephen Garry. New York: Hill and Wang, n.d.

Oboler, Arch and Longstreet, Stephen (eds.). Free World Theatre: Nineteen New Radio Plays. New York: Random House, 1944.

Ramsaye, Terry. A Million and One Nights. New York: Simon and Schuster, 1926.

Reisz, Karel. The Technique of Film Editing. New York: Farrar, Strauss and Cudahy, 1958.

Rotha, Paul. Documentary Film. London: Faber and Faber, Ltd., 1936.

Rotha, Paul and Griffith, Richard. The Film Till Now. London: Spring Books, 1967.

Rotha, Paul, Road, Sinclair and Griffith, Richard. Documentary Film. New York: Hastings House, 1963.

Sheridan, Marion, Owen, Harold, Macrorie, Ken and Marcus, Fred. The Motion Picture and the Teaching of English. New York: Appleton-Century-Crofts, 1965.

Spottiswoode, Raymond. A Grammar of the Film. Berkeley: University of California Press, 1950.

Starr, Cecile. Ideas on Film. New York: Funk and Wagnalls Co., 1951.

Stephenson, Ralph and Debrix, J. R. The Cinema as Art. Great Britain: Cox & Wyman, Ltd., 1965.

Terrett, Dulany. The Signal Corps: The Emergency. Washington, D.C.: U.S. Government Printing Office, 1956.

Thompson, George and Harris, Dixie. The Signal Corps: The Outcome. Washington, D.C.: U.S. Government Printing Office, 1966.

Thompson, George, Harris, Dixie, Oakes, Pauline and Terrett, Dulany. The Signal Corps: The Test. Washington, D.C.: U.S. Government Printing Office, 1957.

Waldron, Gloria. The Information Film. New York: Columbia University Press, 1949.

Articles and Periodicals

Agee, James. Review of the "Army-Navy Screen Magazine," The Nation, (March 4, 1944), 288.

Barnes, Joseph. "Fighting with Information: OWI Overseas," Public Opinion Quarterly, VII (Spring, 1943), 34-45.

Brown, Cecil. "Do You Know What You're Fighting," Colliers (December 11, 1943), 14-15+.

Brown, Thomas. "Army Film Utilization," Business Screen, VII (1945), 41+83.

Byrne, Richard. "Stylistic Analysis of the Film: Notes on a Methodology," Speech Monographs, XXX (March, 1965), 74-78.

Cohen, Emanuel. "Film is a Weapon," Business Screen, VII (1945), 43, 72, 74.

Davidson, Bill. "They Fight With Film," Yank Magazine (March 5, 1943), 20-21.

Grierson, John. "Dramatizing Housing Needs and City Planning," Films, I (November, 1939), 86.

Goldner, Orville. "The Story of Navy Training Films," Business Screen, VI (1945), 29, 32, 84.

Hicks, Orton. "Army Pictures Reach 'Round the World," Business Screen, VII (1945), 53-54, 88.

Horgan, Paul. "The Measure of Army Films," Business Screen, VII (1945), 38-40+87.

Katz, Robert and Katz, Nancy. "Documentary in Transition, Part I: The United States," Hollywood Quarterly, III (1947-48), 425-432.

_____. "Documentary in Transition, Part II: The International Scene and the American Documentary," Quarterly of Radio-Television-Film, IV (1949-50), 51-64.

Lane, R. Kieth. "The O.F.F.," Public Opinion Quarterly, VI (Summer, 1942), 204-220.

Larson, Cedric. "The Domestic Motion Picture Work of the Office of War Information," Hollywood Quarterly, III (1947-48), 434-443.

Liberman, Frank. "A History of Army Photography," Business Screen, VII (1945), 15-17, 94-95.

Maroney, Robert. "Films in the Other Americas," Film News, VI (April, 1945), 2-3.

McMillan, George. "Government Publicity and the Impact of War," Public Opinion Quarterly, V (Fall, 1941), 383-98.

Mayer, Arthur. "Fact into Film," Public Opinion Quarterly, VIII (Summer, 1944), 206-255.

Mock, James and Carson, Cedric. "Public Relations of the U.S. Army," Public Opinion Quarterly, V (June, 1941), 275-82.

Nelson, W. M. "Marines Make Motion Pictures," Film News, III (March, 1942), 2-3.

Waley, H. D. "British Documentaries and the War Effort," Public Opinion Quarterly, VI (Winter, 1942), 604-609.

"Bryan's Films Lead CIAA Program," Film News, III (November 3, 1943), 2.

"Coordinator Shapes War Film Policy," Film News, III (February, 1942),1,8.

"Film Story of OWI Overseas," Film News, V (November, 1944), 3-4.

"Films for Civilian Defense," Film News, III (Late Summer, 1942), 3.

"Health for Defense," Film News, II (May, 1941), 4.

"Military Films," Film News, I (November, 1940), 4-5.

"Navy Trains with Films," Film News, III (November 26, 1942), 4.

"National Defense," Film News, I (October, 1940), 1.

New York Times, February 7, 1943.

"On the Production Line," Business Screen, VII (1945), 24.

"Pep Broadsheet on British Documentary Films," Film News, VI (May, 1945), 8-10.

Time, XXXVIII (August 18, 1941), 36+38.

"U.S. Army Films Go to Public," Film News, IV (November 3, 1943), 3.

Unpublished Material

Byrne, Richard. "German Cinematic Expressionism, 1919-1924." Unpublished Ph.D. dissertation, State University of Iowa, 1962.

Clarke, James. "Signal Corps Army Pictorial Service in World War II, 1 September 1939--15 August 1945." Signal Corps Historical Monograph, Signal Corps Historical File, National Archives, Washington, D.C.

Keppel, Francis. "Study of Information and Education Activity in World War II." Manuscript, Information and Education Division Historical File, National Archives, Washington, D.C.

Kuiper, John. "An Analysis of the Four Silent Films of Sergei Mikhailovich Eisenstein." Unpublished Ph.D. dissertation, State University of Iowa, 1960.

MacCann, Richard. "Documentary Film and Democratic Government: An Administrative History from Pare Lorentz to John Huston." Unpublished Ph.D. dissertation, Harvard, 1951.

Wiley, Raymond. "Why We Fight: The Effort to Indoctrinate Personal Commitment in the American Soldier in World War II." Unpublished seminar paper, Southern Illinois University, 1964. Mimeographed.

The Battle of Britain. Shooting Script. National Archives, Washington, D.C. The "Why We Fight" Series File.

The Battle of China. Shooting Script. National Archives, Washington, D.C. The "Why We Fight" Series File.

The Battle of Russia. Footage Source List. National Archives, Washington D.C. The "Why We Fight" Series File.

The Battle of Russia. Shooting Script. National Archives, Washington, D.C. The "Why We Fight" Series File.

Divide and Conquer. Shooting Script. National Archives, Washington, D.C. The "Why We Fight" Series File.

The Nazis Strike. Shooting Script. National Archives, Washington, D.C. The "Why We Fight" Series File.

Prelude to War. Shooting Script. National Archives, Washington, D.C.

National Archives. Washington, D.C. The "Why We Fight" Series File.

National Archives. Washington, D.C. Frank Capra File.

Prelude to War. Army Orientation Film #1. Bureau of Audio-Visual Instruction, Madison, Wisconsin.

"U.N. Central Training Film Committee Motion Picture Title List." November 21, 1944, Film Section, Library of Congress, Washington, D.C.

DISSERTATIONS ON FILM

An Arno Press Collection

Beaver, Frank Eugene. **Bosley Crowther:** Social Critic of the Film, 1940-1967. First publication, 1974

Benderson, Albert Edward. **Critical Approaches to Federico Fellini's "8½".** First publication, 1974

Berg, Charles Merrell. **An Investigation of the Motives for and Realization of Music to Accompany the American Silent Film, 1896-1927.** First publication, 1976

Blades, Joseph Dalton, Jr. **A Comparative Study of Selected American Film Critics, 1958-1974.** First publication, 1976

Bohn, Thomas William. **An Historical and Descriptive Analysis of the "Why We Fight" Series.** First publication, 1977

Cohen, Louis Harris. **The Cultural-Political Traditions and Developments of the Soviet Cinema: 1917-1972.** First publication, 1974

Dart, Peter. **Pudovkin's Films and Film Theory.** First publication, 1974

Davis, Robert Edward. **Response to Innovation:** A Study of Popular Argument about New Mass Media. First publication, 1976

Facey, Paul W. **The Legion of Decency:** A Sociological Analysis of the Emergence and Development of a Social Pressure Group. First publication, 1974

Feldman, Charles Matthew. **The National Board of Censorship (Review) of Motion Pictures, 1909-1922.** First publication, 1977

Feldman, Seth R. **Evolution of Style in the Early Work of Dziga Vertov.** First publication, 1977

Flanders, Mark Wilson. **Film Theory of James Agee.** First publication, 1977

Fredericksen, Donald Laurence. **The Aesthetic of Isolation in Film Theory: Hugo Munsterberg.** First publication, 1977

Gosser, H. Mark. **Selected Attempts at Stereoscopic Moving Pictures and Their Relationship to the Development of Motion Picture Technology, 1852-1903.** First publication, 1977

James, C. Rodney. **Film as a National Art:** NFB of Canada and the Film Board Idea. First publication, 1977

Karimi, A. M. **Toward a Definition of the American Film Noir (1941-1949).** First publication, 1976

Karpf, Stephen L. **The Gangster Film:** Emergence, Variation and Decay of a Genre, 1930-1940. First publication, 1973

Lounsbury, Myron O. **The Origins of American Film Criticism, 1909-1939.** First publication, 1973

Lyons, Robert J[oseph]. **Michelangelo Antonioni's Neo-Realism:** A World View. First publication, 1976

Lyons, Timothy James, **The Silent Partner:** The History of the American Film Manufacturing Company, 1910-1921. First publication, 1974

McLaughlin, Robert. **Broadway and Hollywood:** A History of Economic Interaction. First publication, 1974

Maland, Charles J. **American Visions:** The Films of Chaplin, Ford, Capra, and Welles, 1936-1941. First publication, 1977

Mason, John L. **The Identity Crisis Theme in American Feature Films, 1960-1969.** First publication, 1977

North, Joseph H. **The Early Development of the Motion Picture, 1887-1909.** First publication, 1973

Paine, Jeffery Morton. **The Simplification of American Life:** Hollywood Films of the 1930's. First publication, 1977

Pryluck, Calvin. **Sources of Meaning in Motion Pictures and Television.** First publication, 1976

Rimberg, John. **The Motion Picture in the Soviet Union, 1918-1952.** First publication, 1973

Sanderson, Richard Arlo. **A Historical Study of the Development of American Motion Picture Content and Techniques Prior to 1904.** First publication, 1977

Sands, Pierre N. **A Historical Study of the Academy of the Motion Picture Arts and Sciences (1927-1947).** First publication, 1973

Shain, Russell Earl. **An Analysis of Motion Pictures about War Released by the American Film Industry, 1939-1970.** First publication, 1976

Snyder, John J. **James Agee:** A Study of His Film Criticism. First publication, 1977

Stuart, Frederic. **The Effects of Television on the Motion Picture and Radio Industries.** First publication, 1976

Wead, George. **Buster Keaton and the Dynamics of Visual Wit.** First publication, 1976

Wolfe, Glenn J. **Vachel Lindsay:** The Poet as Film Theorist. First publication, 1973